SOCIAL WORK, SOCIAL DEVELOPMENT AND SUSTAINABLE DEVELOPMENT

Hajira Kumar
Reader
Dept. of Social Work
Jamia Millia Islamia

2018
Regency Publications
A Division of
Astral International Pvt. Ltd.
New Delhi - 110 002

First Published, 1997
Reprinted, 2018

ISBN: 978-81-86030-38-7 (Hardbound)

Publisher's note:

Every possible effort has been made to ensure that the information contained in this book is accurate at the time of going to press, and the publisher and author cannot accept responsibility for any errors or omissions, however caused. No responsibility for loss or damage occasioned to any person acting, or refraining from action, as a result of the material in this publication can be accepted by the editor, the publisher or the author. The Publisher is not associated with any product or vendor mentioned in the book. The contents of this work are intended to further general scientific research, understanding and discussion only. Readers should consult with a specialist where appropriate.

Every effort has been made to trace the owners of copyright material used in this book, if any. The author and the publisher will be grateful for any omission brought to their notice for acknowledgement in the future editions of the book.

Published by : **Regency Publications**
A Division of
Astral International Pvt. Ltd.
– ISO 9001:2015 Certified Company –
4736/23, Ansari Road, Darya Ganj
New Delhi-110 002
Ph. 011-43549197, 23278134
E-mail: info@astralint.com
Website: www.astralint.com

This is a tribute to the NGOs working effectively in the field of sustainable development.
I believe that the future generations will understand the real worth and significance of their efforts.

PREFACE

It was during 1970s when social workers came out of the narrow image of relief-workers. They started getting involved in the broader issues and gradually shifted over to global problems too. For some time they played the role of propagator and awareness generator in the new fields but later on they also started intervening. In this process, lobbying, agitation and confrontation were also added in the list of social work techniques and skills. In this way, social work marched from social welfare towards social development. Social work has so many connotations. Generally social work is considered a response to the complex situations, which emerge with urbanization and industrialization. It aims at creating a social system where both society and individual are not competitors, rather they are complimentary to each other, which means that society and community should also change and grow to have a better equilibrium between individual and social order. Social development aspires for a society which is more flexible, lively and accommodative, and an individual who is more energetic, confident and responsible. Social work is a close associate of social development. The book in hand throws light on social development not only as a philosophy, but also as a practice module, i.e. 'developmental social work', which has grown under the influence of social development and related theories.

This book also deals with sustainable development because social development remains incomplete without a system of maintaining and sustaining developmental efforts.

Today sustainable development is a concern of physics, chemistry, geology, geography, and action sociology, etc. In this crowd of disciplines, social work is lagging behind. The role of social work and social worker needs redefining in the context of social and sustainable development.

This book covers details regarding the problems in implementing sustainable development. Global issues are discussed briefly but Indian situations are analysed from various angles. Sustainable development has been taken up as an effort to provide protection to the whole planet from droughts, floods, hunger, extinction of species, pollution and social injustice. These are our enemies. Drugs, crime, violence and terrorism are other supportive forces to assist them. Therefore sustainable development is not only a movement rather it is a crusade. In such a situation social workers' activities should play a key role in promoting both social development and sustainable development.

This book is an effort to provide food for thoughts as well as a line to act to those who are interested in these issues. Hopefully, social work students, practitioners and educators will find this a useful reading material.

Sept., 5, 1996
New Delhi

Hajira Kumar
Reader, Dept. of Social Work
Jamia Millia Islamia

ACKNOWLEDGEMENTS

I am deeply indebted to famous environmentalist Shri Sunderlal Bahuguna for the inspiration which I got from his mission. I was also encouraged by his letters which I received during last three years.

I am equally grateful to all the writers and journalists whose informations I have used in this book.

I must also express my obligation to my colleagues in the Department of Social Work, who have helped me in more than one ways.

Let me extend my special thanks to my family members. They have given me moral support for completing this work Above all, I am thankful to my sister Ms. Abida Shakoor who has taken the trouble of going through the text.

CONTENTS

Preface v
Acknowledgements vii

1. Social Development — A Profile 1
Social Development: A Multidimensional Process 2
Social Development: A Multidimensional Issue 3
Salient Features of Social Development 5
Possible Programmes & Activities for Social Development in Indian Context 7
Alleviating and Reducing of Poverty 8
Fight against Exploitation and Oppression 8
Involving and Mobilizing People 9
Utilizing Social Activism, Social Action and Mass Mobilization 9
Lobbying and Advocacy 9
Developing Pressure Groups among Masses 10
Developing Human Resources 10
Fixingup the Target & Priorities 10
Developing Rural Technology and Village Industries 12
Improving Quality of Life and Maximizing the Resources 12
Indicators of Social Development 13
Notes 15

2. The Horizons of Developmental Social Work 17
Developmental Social Work: An Insight 17

Course Content for Social Development Trainees 20
Methods and Techniques for Developmental Social Work 22
Approaches and Objectives of Developmental Social Work 24
Schools of thoughts and Developmental Social Work 27
Notes 27

3. Managing the Fall out of Development in India 29
Side Effects of Developmental Programmes 30
Problems of General Nature 30
Problems Associated with the Faulty Nature of Development 31
Problems Associated with the Well Meaning Development 32
Sustainable Development — Concept and Philosophy 32
Pre-requisites for Sustainable Development 35
Salient Features of Sustainable Development 36
Social Development and Sustainable Developments 40
Notes 42

4. Strategizing Sustainable Development 44
Components of Sustainable Development 45
Strategies for Sustainable Development 46
Analysis of the Issue 47
Contemporary Indian Scenario 50
Notes 52

5. Policy Matters, Political Games and Sustainable Development 54
Some Unrealistic Policies 54
Practice Oriented Philosophy of Sustainable Development 60
Human Rights and Sustainable Development 62
Desirable Activities and Programmes for Government's Consideration 65

Possible Strategies for Social Workers' Intervention 68
Notes 72

6. Sustainable Development: A Different Orientation 74
Bottlenecks in the Process of Sustainable Development 75
Review of the Present Situation 84
Conclusion 85
Notes 87

CHAPTER I

SOCIAL DEVELOPMENT : A PROFILE

The issue of social development had received attention from 1960s. But this does not mean that the concept of development was not in use before. Though for a long time development was identified with economic growth and GNP (Gross National Product) was used as a sole criterion for measuring development".[1]

But after some time the problem regarding the predominance of economic development had been overshadowed by social development "what is called social development is both a part of and the cause of economic development and not a mere follow-up of economic development."[2] This was the view of an economist, otherwise a social worker like M.S. Gore did not take social development as a part of economic development. For him it was the otherway round. "The concept of social development is inclusive of economic development but differs from it in the sense that it emphasises the development of the totality of society in its economic, political, social and cultural aspects .... There are many more areas apart from social or welfare services .... Prominent among these are areas relating to population policy, policy relating to urbanization, industrial location and environmental pollution, policy to regional development, policies of income growth, income distribution and land reforms, policies governing administration and people's participation in planning and in the implementation of plans.

"Social development is thus not a plea for a larger allocation for social and welfare services ... it is really a plea for an integrated view of the scope of development which should embrace development in its varied facets."[3] He further says that any ad-hoc arrangement or service is not social development. Only a long term programme with large scale planning is social development.

Progress, prosperity and peace are the three variables which result in social development but it may be explained a little more elaborately i.e. peace, economic growth, the environmental base, justice and democracy.[4] It is assumed that these factors create situations conducive to social development.

Social Development: A Multi-dimensional Process

There is no doubt that social development cannot be explained so easily. A student of social development and social work must understand social development in a detailed manner with all the intricacies. S.L. Sharma has tried to explain various connotations of social development such as:

1. *Development as economic growth* : This is a common approach where GNP and income per capita are the indicators of development. As a matter of fact the term 'developed' and 'under developed' countries is used on this basis only.
2. *Development as distribution* : The fruits of economic growth should be distributed in a just manner and eventually levelling of income is to be achieved. This will create appropriate atmosphere for development.
3. *Development as improvement in life chances* : UNICEF, ILO, WHO etc. have treated the extent of consumerism, employment and health services as indicators of social development. Overseas Development Council uses the term of 'physical quality of life index' (PQLI) as an indicator which includes life expectancy, death rate, infant mortality rate and literacy rate within it.
4. *Development as liberation from dependency and exploitation* : This aspect includes human right and social justice, which are not easily achieved. It means that not only physical quality but also psycho-social quality of life is equally important.[5]

Social Development: A Multi-dimensional Issue

As a matter of fact, social development is so vast that all the above mentioned variables should be put together. The explanation of M.S. Gore (1973) is not very different from the findings of World Summit on Social Development (1995). The findings of the World Summit on Social Development have been discussed in the news letter of ASSWI. "The three core issues, enhancement of social integration, particularly of marginalised and disadvantaged groups, alleviation and reduction of poverty and expansion of productive employment (and their extension in primary health care, basic education, safe drinking water, nutrition programme, family planning services and drug control as priority concerns) selected for the Summit are indeed important and also inter-related."[6] A student of social work would understand that these are age old issues; they are well understood but have not been solved so far. And obviously they are becoming more and more complicated. Indian planners and policy makers are trying to work on these issues (the latest effort is the improved 20 point programme). We cannot claim that the World Summit has given any new idea. However, the most important point is the concern expressed for global equality which means a change in the life style of the developed countries. They should be reducing their luxuries in favour of the developing countries. After the fall of former Soviet Union it is surprising that the welfare states are tilting towards equality and social justice even more. According to R.R. Singh, "The Gandhian ideal of austere, authentic, basic need-oriented and non-consumerist societies becomes relevant."[7] Another point raised in the Summit, was the emphasis laid on people's participation which means that the difference of real need and felt need would be over. They will not be contrary to each other. Programmes and plans should be participatory at every stage, to the extent that, beyond a point even 'human resource development' becomes commodification of human beings and is against the spirits of authentic social development.[8] In other words people should not be forced to be trained in a particular field which is not their choice.

Even before the World Summit, social development was defined by the ASSWI almost on the same lines. "Social Development is a process of systematic change (values, attitudes, institutions and practices) purposefully initiated through the instruments of social policy and planning for the enhancement of the levels of living and quality of life of the mass of people especially the weaker section in an eco-friendly socially just and participatory environment."[9]

To make it more practical the World Summit on Social Development has made some declarations and commitments. Major of them are listed below:

1. Levelling the incomes of rich and poor in order to promote social justice.
2. Alleviating poverty and generating employment.
3. Working for global compact plan for social development.
4. Fighting against global problems like drug mafia and terrorism.
5. Fighting against the discrimination on the basis of gender, race, religion, age or disability.
6. Protecting the disadvantaged groups and sections.
7. Providing special assistance for social development programmes and working to promote public and private assistance.
8. Integrating poverty reduction and gender equity objectives into the programme of structural adjustment by using social-impact assessment and other relevant methods to ensure a greater focus upon issues of social development and basic human needs.
9. Improving the international economic environment to improve international financial assistance for helping underdeveloped countries.[10]

It is needless to say that, all this discussion is making social development further ambiguous. It is natural because "Social Development has been called a perspective, a practice model and a movement. It is all these."[11] This is the claim of Caryl Abraham and others in their 'Manual for Social Development Practice'. The same manual further describes "Social Development is based on positive, human and people oriented development in society .... Social development is a practical approach and can be used at individual, family, community and national and international levels. The social development worker should be able to practice at all these levels. This is called Practice Mobility ...."[12] The basic principles of social development are human dignity, equality, social justice and equitable distribution of resources. These concepts are not separate. They depend upon each other. Equality is not possible without a firm belief in human dignity. If equality and dignity are present for all individuals, social justice follows. Social development values cooperation over competition, collectivism over individualism and integration over segregation among people.

Salient Features of Social Development

With this explanation certain points about social development are getting clearer, such as:

1. Social development is a programme as well as a movement, approach and method of treating any broad-based issue. Campaigning and mass mobilization are required much more in social development in comparison to social welfare.
2. Social development may not provide direct (here and now) type of readymade services with immediate solution of the problems. It means long-term planning which is based on 'investing' in people, environment and social system.
3. Indirect and long-term strategies are adopted due to the approach of attacking the roots of the problems and needs. It is presupposed that social problems are complex phenomena. Many problems which appear to be serious social evils are actually off-shoots of the main problem such as 'Sati', 'widow remarriage restriction' and 'dowry system' are the off-shoots of the lower status of women. In the same way child labour, mal-nutrition and slums are associated with poverty and unemployment. In order to work against these problems we have to plan an attack upon the very roots.
4. Collective problems and general needs are the main focus of social development because individual problems, such as psychosomatic bodyache, sibling rivalry and nail-

biting cannot be the areas of operation for a developmental worker. He would feel more interested in issues like disarmament, refugees' displacement, ecological imbalance, and gender and racial discrimination.

5. Lobbying and mass mobilization are essentially required in social development because participation, involvement, and contribution of people who are going to be benefitted are needed more, therefore the activities are usually based on the felt needs. But it does not mean that awareness generation is not a part of the developmental approach, clients' awareness about the technological advancement or more scientific choices in life is also a primary activity in developmental programmes. The difference is simple. The programme will not be imposed on the masses as it has been done in the government sponsored welfare programmes where planners and beneficiaries have been two distinct groups.
6. In the field of social development community organisation and social action are more appropriate methods in place of case work, counselling, and group work. Involvement of the professionals from other related disciplines is also welcomed. These professionals may be police officers, bankers, government servants, policy makers, town planners, legal advisors or politicians etc. For massive action programmes mere social work is a small weapon. Therefore a support group in the broader context is required.
7. The 'goody goody' approach in social work is a bit outdated now; the developmental social worker has to fight against:
   (a) Criminals who use slums and slum-dwellers for their selfish motives. They use them as labourers and helpers for criminal activities.
   (b) Police and administrative authorities who are corrupt and let the crime flourish under their nose.
   (c) Traditional system which is based on unscientific practices and beliefs. It is necessary because new beliefs, strategies and practices cannot be introduced unless old order winds off.
   (d) Politics and politicians, because they, sometime, cre-

ate an atmosphere where social development remains only a lip service. They at times encourage corrupt practices in the name of social development, sometimes they want to avoid social development programmes because they come in the way of their unethical and corrupt practices.

(e) Traditional type of social welfare workers who believe that these type of off-beat radical activities which developmental social workers render are ultimately going to harm the profession. As Pathak has said "There is a strong and vocal section of social work educators who fear that the identity of professional social work, so pains-takingly built over several decades is about to be lost in our zeal for social change and development."[13] He further says, "A majority of social work educators are highly sceptical of our legitimacy and competence to prepare social workers for the radical confrontationalist practice in the field."[14]

As a result of this controversy there is a problem of non-availability of course curriculum in the field of social development. Moreover, it is too high an expectation to imagine that a two year programme would prepare a student in the traditional role of ameliorative-rehabilitative function and side by side for catalysts role of developmental functions.

Possible Programmes and Activities for Social Development in Indian Context

A student of social work feels that it is easy to implement possible activities and programme under social development because social development approach is more relevant for Asian and African countries. India is progressing no doubt but the rate of progress is far from being satisfactory, therefore, some social development activities which may be suitable to Indian context are listed below.

Alleviating and Reducing of Poverty

A war against poverty and unemployment was always considered a priority for social development worker. Pathak has quoted Dudley Seer for explaining the original concept, indicators and objectives of social development. "The questions to ask about a country's development are therefore, what has been happening to poverty? What has been happening to unemployment? What has been happening to inequality? If all three of these have declined from high level then beyond doubt this has been a period of development for the country concerned. If one or two of these central problems have been growing worse, especially if all the three have, it would be strange to call the result, development even if per capita income doubled."[15] It is needless to say that the developmental social worker works with the root cause of poverty and unemployment besides working for the individuals or groups victimised by poverty and unemployment.

Fighting against Exploitation and Oppression

There is a controversy about the approach as well as programme which may be covered in the scope of social development. As Pathak remarks "Even among the prochangers there are divergent views on the inclusion and exclusion of officially sponsored programmes as part of social development such as family planning and population control, ICDS, community health programme etc.... another section strongly differs from this view advocating a radical stance by social workers with reference to the issues of social injustice, exploitation and oppression (including gender related discrimination and oppression). The latter group includes those whose ideology ranges from Freire's conscientisation to pro-Marxist ideologies that aim to bring about a major structural change not excluding confrontation and conflict as a part of their strategies."[16] In this description certain issues need more clarification eg. are the two set of programmes totally different? Are those who are working in the first category of programme not agent of social change? Are oppressor and oppressed always two different groups or oppressed some times gladly accept oppression and even glorify it (as it is in the case of lower status of women). If it is so, then developmental social worker has to fight against the clients' ideologies themselves too. But the argument may be extended if we say that the acceptance of oppressing behaviour is due to the social conditioning of the mind since early days.

Involving and Mobilizing People

Awareness generation, conscientisation and then deep involvement of the people is an important factor; it may not be programme in itself but it is definitely the first step of all the programmes. Bedi has rightly remarked, "Unless people do not develop some tension regarding their existing sub-human existence and a life of deprivation, they cannot be energized and activated to strive for better standard of living."[17]

Utilizing Social Activism, Social Action and Mass Mobilization

Campaigning and mass movement are the usual techniques of initiating social development programmes. Bringing about change faster than the usual rate (but not revolution) is one of the objectives of social development because social development is a perspective, a practice mode and a movement.[18] According to this explanation the programme and activities involved in social development cannot be listed out completely. Besides that, more important aspect is not the programme content but the treatment which is given to various issues.

Lobbying and Advocacy

Initiating social development is a massive task. For launching social development activities, social workers are not all in all, they neither develop a band of grass-root workers nor are they the leaders of the team. They work just as one section of the whole working group which should include political leaders, industrialists, advocates, town planners and policy makers etc. because the work starts much before the problem arises. For this reason lobbying and advocacy are two important skills which in India are not used at present with the full force. Due to the cost of mass media devices, a lot of money is required for investment; which of course is justified because social development programmes are long-term and large-scale programmes. In a good developmental project money should not be a problem because so many professionals work jointly.

Developing Pressure Groups among Masses

For all such projects, planning and policy making is essential. It is not possible that all the development workers start working as planner or policy makers. They prepare pressure groups. In this way a developmental social worker contributes in policy making because it is the approach and treatment of the worker which makes a particular activity development oriented or just welfare oriented.

Developing Human Resources

One of the basic tasks is the investment in people (human resource development) which includes providing atleast minimum acceptable level of education, health and nutrition. As a matter of fact World Bank is working in that area. In developing countries World Bank is working with the problems such as mal-nutrition, population policy, universal primary education, poverty and unemployment. This is their way of investment in people.[19]

Fixingup the Target and Priorities

For all the programmes and activities the first and the foremost task is the fixation of the target. For global issues this is even more important because in those cases efforts ascertaining root cause may create further confusion e.g. in the case of poverty eradication, developed countries have to sacrifice some of their resources for the sake of less fortunate countries. At present they are not having this approach and it is difficult to sacrifice resources and comforts willingly which they have been enjoying since long. They must also be thinking that these comforts and luxuries are their right. If any redistribution is initiated, then many of them will not take it as 'development' for them. The global in justice is like this:

Distribution of economic activity, 1991
(percentage of world total)

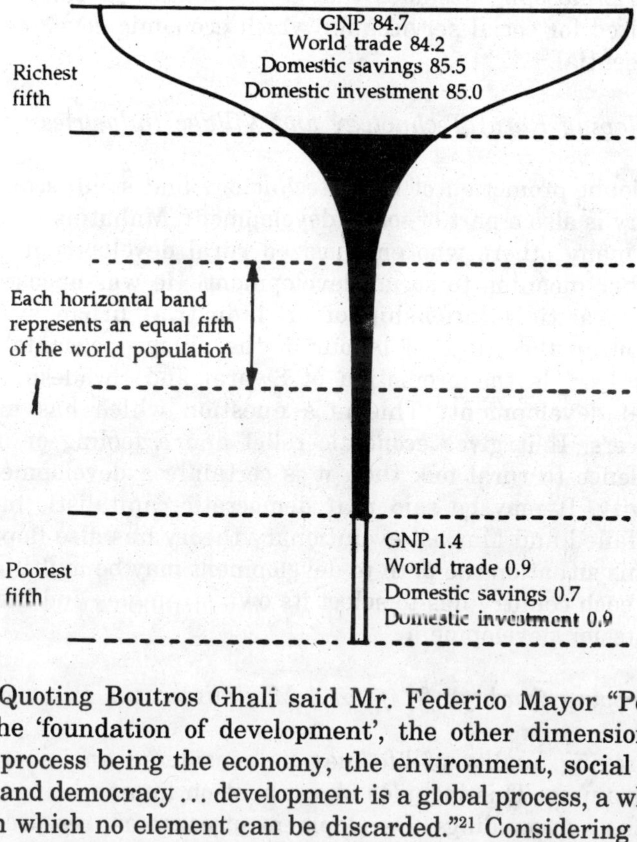

Quoting Boutros Ghali said Mr. Federico Mayor "Peace is the 'foundation of development', the other dimension of the process being the economy, the environment, social justice and democracy ... development is a global process, a whole from which no element can be discarded."[21] Considering this it is not a chance that most of the underdeveloped countries are also having pathetic, violent experience both politically and socially. In the present situation the vast gap between rich and poor nations make the poor nations almost colonies for the developed rich countries. Poor nations can hardly spend on the items essential for social development. There is a universally accepted pattern of investment on human resources. Pathak has explained them in detail. He says that Social development includes programmes for universal literacy or primary education, comprehensive preventive health measures, treatment and control of contagious diseases (like leprosy, poliomyelitis), housing, family planning and preservation of ecological balance. Moreover, social development philosophy assumes that a substantial investment is required for social services for which economic development is essential.[22]

Developing Rural Technology and Village Industries

No doubt promotion of rural technology and small scale industry is also a part of social development. Mahatma Gandhi and many others who emphasized rural development gave another meaning to social development. He was opposed to the parasitic relationship of an industrial urban system exploiting the fruits of labour of the village peasants and artisans.[23] Is the promotion of Swaraj and Swadeshi also social development? This is a question which has many answers. If it gives economic relief and a feeling of independence to rural folk then it is certainly a developmental activity. It may be said that democratic capitalistic model has failed and Marxist evolutionary theory has also flopped. In this situation the path to development may be multilinear and each country has to select its own strategies and instruments for development.

Improving Quality of Life and Maximizing the Resources

Improving quality of life may be considered an important programme. This includes investment on human beings and on the surroundings. Development of economic resources is also a part of improving quality of life. In this context it is needless to say that maximization of resources is not going to be at the cost of environmental exploitation. In that case it will not be 'development'. Eco-friendly attitude is a must for all developmental strategies.

By and large all the above mentioned activities and programmes are included in developmental approach though many more keep on joining time to time.

Indicators of Social Development

It is obvious that social development is a long term and large scale strategy. It also involves lot of expenditure, therefore all these efforts should be in the right direction. Social development as a method and field of practice is still vague and unclear, therefore some indicators must be fixedup to measure the extent of achievement. Simple criteria like life expectancy, literacy rate, income and consumption per capita are definitely considered the main criteria but some refined and exclusive indicators have also been developed, such as Human Development Index (HDI) which consists of GNP per capita, life expectancy and mean years of schooling. Moreover 'public spending' on development is also significant in this regard. In order to make it perfect, four types of ratios are suggested to measure the involvement of society and state in human development, such as percentage of national income going into public expenditure (25 p.c. is approved), social allocation ratio (SAR) percentage of public expenditure allotted on social service items such as health care and education (40 p.c. approved), the social priority ratio (SPR) expenditure. From social allocation for priority needs e.g. basic education, primary health etc. (50 p.c. is suggested) and the human expenditure ratio which should be approximately 5 p.c. of national income. Above 5 p.c. of the national income is high level of expenditure; between 3–5 p.c. of national income is low level of expenditure.[24]

These indicators may be sufficient but United Nation's Universal Declaration of Human Right Convention 1992 and the International Covenants on Civil and Political Rights alongwith Economic, Social and Cultural Rights have given some other indicators such as Right of the child, and Elimination of All Forms of Discrimination Against Women. Convention on the Political Right of Women are also important indicators. The status of human rights in a particular country is indicated by the Ratification of International Instruments.[25] It is pre-supposed that high level of social and human development is closely linked with maximization of human freedom.

UNICEF has chosen another largely accepted parameter of development 'U5MR' which means mortality rate under 5 years of age in a particular year for every thousand births in that year. According to them less than 70 deaths under 5 year is an indicative of development. India has 152 (39th from bottom), Afghanistan has 304, Sweden has U5MR of 7 only.[26]

No doubt social development scenario in India is difficult to be evaluated. Freedom House a research organisation has rated India as a 'free country having political rights and political participation, civil liberties, protection from political violence of military rule and balance between military and non-military expenditure. India has a better status in comparison to Afghanistan, Bangladesh, Bhutan, Nepal and Pakistan. Sri Lanka is equivalent in this regard.[27]

On the other hand some people feel that India has not progressed, rather regressed, e.g. Sethi feels that IRDP, RLEGP, DPAP, and NREP do not reach the poor, only elites among the downtrodden utilize every such privilege. He says, "There is a definite long-term inverse relationship between economic growth and absolute poverty.... The most tragic aspect of the poverty debate is that it cynically conceals the fact that growth without redistribution accentuates poverty.

"Official estimates ignore the following factors: high incidence of disease which pushes below the poverty line those who are above it...., discrimination within the family against girls and women, substitution of the needs of the poor in times of social and other crises; poor quality of food,...."[28]

Besides this, Chengappa and others have discussed some parameters about urban set-up such as: availability of electricity, tap water and toilet as criteria for development.

In this context it would be wiser if we evaluate every achievement, programme wise as well as area wise (like country, state, district or locality). There has been considerable difference among various areas and programmes both. This means that evaluation of every programme should be done on local basis, national and state picture would be confusing.

One more criterion which is indigenous is also worth mentioning i.e. girl child mortality ratio or number of female for 1000 male. There is a lot of difference in girl child mortality ratio between developed and depressed states in India. It is interesting to note that availability of female per 1000 male is 941 in rural areas, and 893 in urban areas. Does this mean that the status of women is even lower in the cities ?[29]

With the above discussion it is clear that there are many criteria to measure social development and none of them is insignificant, moreover they are interlinked also. All of them should be gradually achieved when the journey for social development starts.

NOTES

1. Rama S. Pandey, "Development Peace and Human Rights in South Asia", *The Indian Journal of Social Work,* Vol. LIV No. 4, Tata Institute of Social Sciences, Bombay, October 1993, p. 536
2. V.K.R.V. Rao quoted by Mirza Ahmed, "Social Development and Human Rights", in *Journal of Social Work,* Vol. VIII (Lucknow; Dept. of Social Work), p. 4
3. M.S. Gore, *Some Aspects of Social Development* (TISS Deptt. of Social Work & University of Hongkong, August 15 1973), p. 10
4. *Population and Development* Review Documents U.N. Agenda for Development Emerging Infectious Disease threat, Vol. 20 No. 3 (New York: Population Council, September 1994), p. 683.
5. Based on S.L. Sharma's Development, *Socio Cultural Dimension* (Jaipur, Rawat Publication 1986, p. 3–6).
6. R.R. Singh "World Summit on Social Development: Some Reflections" *Newsletter* ASSWI Vol. No. 1, Spring 1995, p. 1.
7. *Ibid* p. 1.
8. *Ibid* p. 6.
9. ASSWI *Newsletter*, Vol. No. 2 (Delhi, DSSW, 1994) Autumn.
10. *World Summit for Social Development* "Consensus Growing on Summit" U.N. Publication Copenhegen, March 1995.
11. Caryl Abraham and others, *A Manual for Social Development Practice* (Canada: Toronto Canadian Scholar Press and Colombo National Institute of Social Development, 1994), p. 2.
12. *Ibid.*
13. "Social Development and Social Work some Unsolved Issues" Shankar Pathak in R.K. Nayak & H.Y. Siddiqui, *Social Work*

and Social Development (New Delhi: Gitanjali Publishing House, 1989) p. 7.

14. *Ibid.* p. 8.
15. Dudley Seers quoted by Pathak, in *Social Welfare—An Evolutionary and Developmental Perspective* (Delhi: Macmillan India Ltd., 1981), p. 152.
16. S.H. Pathak, "Social Development and Social Work some Unresolved Issues", Nayak and Siddiqui, *Social Work and Social Development* (New Delhi: Gitanjali Publishing House, 1989), p. 7 & 8.
17. M.S. Bedi, *Social Development and Social Work* (Udaipur: Himanshu Publication, 1994), p. 22.
18. Abraham, *A Manual for Social Development Practice*, p. 2.
19. The World Bank, *Investing in People: The World Bank in Action* (Washington, D.C. 1995), Preface.
20. *Searching New Development Strategies* Policy paper I MOST Copenhagen, March 1995.
21. Extract from the speech given by Mr. Federico Mayor Director General of UNESCO at the symposium *What happened to Development* UNESCO, Paris, 18–19 June 1994.
22. Pathak, "Social Development" *Encyclopaedia of Social Work in India,* Vol. III (New Delhi: Publication Division, 1987), p. 58.
23. *Ibid.*
24. U.N. Development Programme 1991 quoted by Rama S. Pandey, "Development Peace and Human Right in South Asia" in *The Indian Journal of Social Work* Vol. LN No. 4 (TISS October, 1983) p. 539.
25. U.N. Human Rights — 1992 quoted by Rama S. Pandey, "Development Peace and Human Rights", p. 542.
26. U.N.I. quoted by Mirza R. Ahmed, "Social Development & Human Right", in *Journal of Social Work* Vol. VIII (Lucknow: Deptt. of Social Work, 1991) p. 5.
27. Freedom House quoted by Rama S. Pandey, p. 543.
28. J.D. Sethi, 'Poverty in India' quoted by Mirza R. Ahmed, in "Social Development & Human Right" *Journal of Social Work* (Lucknow: Deptt. of Social Work, 1991), p. 4.
29. Census of India 1991, Paper 2, Series 1 quoted by D. Paul Chowdhry, *Women Welfare and Development* (New Delhi: Inter India Publications, 1992), p. 28.

CHAPTER II

THE HORIZONS OF DEVELOPMENTAL SOCIAL WORK

It has already been discussed that social development is not a concern of social work alone. As a matter of fact social development has been often discussed by sociologists and economists; for example S.L. Sharma wrote, *Development : Socio-cultural Dimension* (1986), R.D. Sharma, *Development Administration* (1992) and *Social Development in the Third World* was edited by the J.G.M. Milharst & M. Klatter (1985) etc. Social Development has attracted planners and policy makers much before the summit in Copenhagen. An organised effort started for social development in 1973-74 in Bangkok located United Nations Social Development Division when they changed the name of ECAFE (Economic Commission for Asia and Far East) into ESCAP (Economic & Social Commission for Asia and the Pacific). This clearly indicates the change of thrust from economic development to social development.

Developmental Social Work: An Insight

There is no doubt that social work practice is getting influenced by the growing philosophy of social development though some senior social work professionals like M.S. Gore have been quite sceptical about the union of social development and social work profession. At one place he writes, "The relationship of social work to social development is still undefined and in an exploratory stage. In India, social workers have tried in the past to be involved in some of the programmes of social development with only partial success. In the 1950s when the community development movement was launched by the government, social workers sought an entry into the movement but the only area where they could establish themselves as an important professional group was the area of training, particularly, the training of social education officers."[1]

These types of apprehensions continued for a long time but social development strategies grew. As a matter of fact during 1960s some thinkers developed the concept of social welfare services as normal and front line activity of the society which is not a special favour but is a matter of right for the citizens. It is not a 'doze' for any ailment. It is a general 'nutrition' which every one must have. At that time some features of social development became visible. Pathak feels that social development, grew as a result of an attempt to link social welfare to the emerging trends in planned national development programme. At that time "a new term developmental social welfare was coined .... However, it was very soon discovered that while the Christening ceremony was over no one had seen the baby. What did this new baby look like? Thus it was that, Kulkarni was invited to describe the characteristics of developmental social warfare in Nairobi in 1974."[2] Here Kulkarni described the following characteristics of developmental social welfare.

1. Institutional change i.e. not maintaining status quo.
2. Functional efficiency and careful use of resources.
3. Preparation of the resources for planned social change.[3]

Here it must be mentioned that inspite of these early efforts the areas of social development appeared to be out of bound to social workers for sometimes. Specially areas like poverty eradication, cooperatives, low cost housing, refugees' migration, consumer forums and environment preservation do not provide sufficient opportunities for the traditional social worker to show his skills. The reasons are quite a few. Let us make a list of some of these major factors such as:

1. The traditional and conventional image of a social worker which is of a provider, relief worker and fund raiser,

does not coincide with the requirements of a development worker.

2. Still social workers try to stay away from broad based, macro level programme. On the other hand they attach special importance to counselling, case work, problem solving and crisis intervention.
3. Management and administrative skills are usually not taught to social work trainees (Dept. of Social Work J.M.I. has included this task in its field work requirement recently) which are required for developmental social work.[4]
4. In big cities social workers are growing with urban bias. They also get jobs easily. Therefore they can avoid the experience of rural and tribal life altogether. As a result they do not prepare themselves to work for innovative and challenging projects.
5. The idea of mass mobilization does not appear appealing to the traditional social workers. They feel that their efforts will be diluted because they believe in small group and face to face contacts.

These were the main hurdles before social workers but in the beginning of 1980s developmental social work became more and more popular. Social workers and social work educators came to the conclusion that working with micro level and small issues can not even solve the problem of individual clients unless larger, national or international issues are solved because individual problems are the offshoots of social problems. Therefore, slowly, some of them changed their thrust. At this time with a little apprehension developmental social work was recognized as a bonafide stream in social work profession.

Tasks before developmental social work were massive and social workers with their expertise in case work and group work were not in a position to work as developmental social worker but later they realised "the more fundamental task in India and other developing countries is needed to bring about radical changes in the social and economic systems with their in-built injustices and imbalances. Hence, that social workers role as a change agent is to be less with individuals and more with total social and economic fabric of the country through positive, purposeful and even aggressive participation in social development to change the economic and social contours of the country. In this task, skills in social planning, social policy analysis and formulation become very important."[5] It was a timely realization. Social work started enriching its self with new horizons. The above mentioned Pathak and Jacob's statements explain that social development is now accepted as a part of social work profession. Today we see that inspite of being a little vague the developmental model of social work is becoming popular among professional social workers. The reasons are many such as:

1. It looks closer to socialistic thoughts which are more fascinating for the people of underdeveloped countries.
2. It is also appreciated by the feminist organisations because it takes up gender issues since developmental social workers want to adopt the approach of no injustice and no discrimination.
3. It has inter-disciplinary nature, therefore people from other disciplines and fields are also getting interested in this comparatively new approach.
4. There has been a lot of international support and appreciation for developmental activities and programmes.
5. This is a comparatively new philosophy and appears to be more innovative and challenging, as a result, many people are finding it more exciting. Its all embracing canvas covers all sorts of programmes.
6. Social activism and social action are the main methods in social development which are highly appreciated by the young, enthusiastic professionals due to their inherent militant zeal.

Course Content for Social Development Trainees

Today social development is no more a prohibited field rather it is an appreciated area for social worker. In 1981 Gore felt that social development area should not be exploited (explored) by social workers. It is only a tertiary area for social worker but within fifteen years things have changed a lot. Report of the Curriculum Development Centre in Social Work

Education (prepared by TISS and sponsored by UGC in 1990) has taken up social development as a part of social work.

Today contemporary social work provides knowledge base for the students of developmental social work, the course includes philosophy of social development and related concepts like sustainable development and people's development. It also provides social science content, more than what is provided in the traditional social work because interdisciplinary approach is adopted. Moreover methods, techniques and skills for the field work are taught. Social justice, human rights, needs and problems in the society and social welfare administration are also included. Welfare state its programmes and government efforts are integral part of it. Sufficient knowledge about voluntary action is also considered essential. The issues like underdevelopment, scarcity, poverty and deprivation are given prominence.

The courses of traditional social work and developmental social work are quite similar but approaches like social action and integrated method are given importance in social development. Moreover, radical, Marxist, feminist and Gandhian approaches are given front line position in developmental social work.

Here, it should be mentioned that traditional concern of social workers such as human factor consideration, individualization and warmth of professional relationship is not ignored.

Vera Mehta gives her opinion in connection with the area of developmental social work. She feels, besides the regularly accepted areas . "... Some of the new contents that need to be included are the following:

(i) System analysis (ii) group dynamics and inter personal relationships (iii) administrative processes and organizational operations (iv) social community dynamics and dynamics of change (v) finding of theoretical formulational and empirical studies (vi) social work method of inter personal intervention (vii) social and personal dysfunction covering what are enhancing and what are endangering social development process."[6]

Moreover, the system of teaching should also be innovative. Besides lectures, demonstration, paper presentation, small group discussions, case studies, role plays, group exercises, workshops, films, and discussion on creative literature should be used. Teaching in this field should have more students' participation. Regular field work experiences should also be discussed in the classroom. Students should be given to understand that western theories and western literature may not be all the time applicable in Indian situation. Therefore their own experiences in the field are also quite valuable. Field work content in the courses should be more intense both qualitatively and quantitatively. Innovative field work projects which are working in remote areas must be visited and observed, for this purpose the general pattern of twice a week field work must be changed. Field work may be started in blocks i.e. one month teaching and one month field work. Eight weeks block field work must be fixed in a remote area. In developmental social work urban bias must be avoided. The students should be mentally prepared to face negative reactions. Confrontation is not impossible because one section may feel threatened due to institutional and structural changes. In field work, macro realities should be studied and helping process must include mass mobilization.

Methods and Techniques for Developmental Social Work

It has already been made clear that almost all the primary and auxilliary methods of social work are required in social development. But community organisation, social action and integrated methods are used more often. The reason of this preference is the nature of social development approach which usually involves mass mobilization. It has been said that social development is a perspective, practice mode, and a movement; therefore, sometime the methods of working with large groups such as addressing public gatherings and rallies are used and the traditional concept of 'small groups' and 'face to face relationship' the worker has to forgo for sometime.

Community organisation has been explained by Surendra Singh "As a method of social work, community organisation is concerned with improvement of social provisions for some disadvantaged and disenfranchised population and for enhancement of social relationship to develop greater capacity in some larger population to deal with common problem".[7] This explains that community oganisation is a rational choice for social development oriented social worker.

On the other hand social action is also an appropriate method for social development. R.R. Singh says with full force "Social action is an essential component of developmental social work practice, which can not be subsumed by the holy trinity of the so called primary methods of professional social work, nor can it be adequately covered through a single course."[8] He further says "practice experience in this area is either non-existent or limited through planned or accidental encounters."[9] Social action is no doubt an appreciable method for developmental work. The origin of human problems, needs and maladjustment is studied with the help of socioeconomic and political environment and not through psychology and personality of the individual. Instead of improving the personality, developmental social work aims at improving the social system. In fact launching an issue base movement with a subdued political tinge and mass resource mobilization is the most popular method for developmental social work.

Besides this, the general integrated method of social work is also useful for developmental social work. Here for a particular project, programme or movement (social action), the worker uses all the primary or secondary methods at the same time because he tries to attack on a problem or an issue from all the corners.

The usual processes in developmental social work are identification, articulation, persuation, mobilisation, prevention, conflict, confrontation, competition, experimentation, empowerment and institutionalization. The skills are quite similar to those of the usual social work skills such as observation, communication and empathy. Moreover, organisational skills, evaluation skills, crisis management and public relation skills are used time to time.

It is evident from the above discussion that the developmental social work's methods and skills are not very different from the already established skills of social work profession, only the emphasis is somewhat more over certain methods and techniques but other methods are also recognised and given due importance. Statham says " ... since adjusting, therapeutic, amelioration, clinical social control functions are increasingly being found inadequate and therefore the emphasis is being placed on preventive developmental and liberative function".[10] R.R. Singh adds to that " ... however it needs to be clarified that developmental social work does not exclude an amelioration or therapeutic approach. Its holistic framework, on the contrary, treats clinical-preventive-developmental dimensions as a continuum and as inter-related phases of an integrated approach to human service."[11]

The canvas of developmental social work practice is very vast, therefore many devoted and daring workers are required. Naturally with this approach one to one relationship can not flourish. All embracing methods which are used for social development indicate that developmental activities are basically inter-disciplinary efforts. They need many other professionals for a massive action.

It is obvious that developmental social work will develop new methods and techniques with the passing time because it is growing as an indigenous philosophy in Indian contexts too.

Approaches and Objectives of Developmental Social Work

There have been some variations regarding the concept of achievements in developmental social work. There is no doubt that developmental social work aims at developing the society with all its sections and with the basic unit i.e. individual. The problem arises when we say that developmental social work is based on mass mobilization. Because in this process it is possible that the elities or leaders among downtrodden take the lead as well as the lion's share of the fruits of development. As a result, inspite of achievement, masses may be deprived of that.

Moreover, if it is going to be a socio-political movement then the involvement of various power pockets in the country or in any particular area is inevitable. In that case it is quite possible that the whole project/movement is diffused and (perhaps) misguided, because in that situation the achievements would be stepping stones for political gains.

Thirdly, it is not possible to control the movement or radical activities in social action beyond a point. Some reformers may feel that there is nothing wrong in it. As J.P. Narayan commented, "When a revolutionary movement is on, its aims should not remain limited to whatever they were at the beginning, but taking advantage of the revolutionary atmosphere, they should be widened to cover as many fields of social life as possible."[12] This approach is acceptable for a socio-political movement but a plan of action for social development oriented social work activities must not be unguided. However quite often things move very fast in developmental social work and the social worker can not control them fully. In that case desired goals may not be achieved.

All these problems are there, partly, due to broad nature of the developmental social work. In this situation it is important to ascertain the approaches and objectives. These objectives focus at:

1. Developing and mobilizing internal or external resources and collaborating with the masses for a movement/project.
2. Planning carefully institutional and structural changes in the old social system. These changes should attack the roots of the social problems and not the offshoots.
3. Influencing, modifying and developing social policies with the help of pressure groups of interested sections of public and co-professionals.
4. Creating harmony with the nature and with all the sections of fellow human beings. This may be deemed as the underlying current of developmental social work.
5. Creating equal opportunities but supporting marginalized and socially handicapped sections. This includes raising voice against the faulty planning by the government. As Warren Christopher, former U.S. Deputy Secretary of State adds in human rights list "...the right to the

fulfilment of such vital needs as food, shelter, health care and education. The stage of a nation's economic development will obviously affect the fulfilments of this right .... This right can be violated by a government's action or inaction, for example, when a government diverts vast proportion of its country's limited resources to corrupt officials or to the creation of luxuries for an elite while millions endure hunger and deprivation."[13]

6. Fighting against poverty and unemployment. It is meaningful if we can control corruption with it because poorest of the poor or the most deserving people will not be able to touch the fruit of social development otherwise. Food for work, community development programme and IRDP have not been so successful. This is all due to corruption and mismanagement.[14] Now the recent programme for urban poor is yet to be monitored or evaluated by various bodies.
7. Organising public interest litigation. It is another objective of the developmental social work. Justice Krishna Iyer has put forth his point of view that there is a need for a "second freedom struggle to protect human rights, make the government responsive and responsible, judges active and justice available to all."[15] Public interest litigation indicates a situation where the victims are so much suppressed that they can not even raise their voice for demanding justice, the developmental social worker empathises and raises voice against injustice on their behalf.
8. Launching various programmes of environment preservation: It includes fighting against both traditional (e.g. pollution of Ganges water) and modern (Bhopal gas tragedy) environmental problems. This may include mass media mobilization, specially when the big powers are exploiting developing countries e.g. Methyl Isocyanate was not produced and stored in Britain for last ten years and it is controlled by machines and computers in developed countries even if it is produced. But only in India it was handled manually, produced and stored in bulk. All this is sponsored and managed by the firms of the developed countries. This shows that big powers are so

much careless about under developed countries that they would start a factory without safeguards. But a developmental social worker mobilizes masses over this issue. It may take the turn of a mass movement.

Schools of Thought and Developmental Social Work

As a matter of fact developmental social work may be some thing comparatively new but social development and social 'reform facing confrontation' is quite an old experience. Right from the emergence of Buddhism we can trace the history of protest movements. In an organized manner radical, Marxist and Gandhian social work, proceed on the lines of developmental social work. These theories promote innovative, broadbased and long term activities in social work. We can not ignore other theories too, such as systems theory, existentialism and problem solving theory. Developmental social work has taken 'sub-systems' and 'universe' etc. term from systems theory, the ideal of self worth and freedom of choice are taken from existentialism and the problem solving theory provides a social base for all the problems.

In Indian context, the role of developmental social work is crucial. It is good that the early planners were not ignorant about it. Pathak has written at one place that Nehru's conception of social development was based on socialism and it influenced planning for economic development on the Soviet model.[16] Developmental social work includes certain issues such as ecofeminism, gender and race discriminations and the problem of human rights in a pluralistic society etc. These problems make it closer to radical theory which make human suffering and misery a social responsibility. Social base has been utilized in Marxists theories. The concept of 'peaceful confrontation and resistence' brings developmental social work closer to Gandhian approach too. In actual practice developmental social work remains under the shadow of many theories; even then it is growing as a philosophy in itself.

NOTES

1. M.S. Gore, *Some Aspects of Social Development* (Bombay: TISS 1973), p. 37.
2. S.H. Pathak, *Social Welfare* (New Delhi: Macmillan India Ltd., 1981), p. 161.
3. See for details Pathak, *Social Welfare*, Chapter 10.
4. A.C. Almanzor, "Social Work Curriculum for Development", in Jacob (ed.), *Social Development Perspective* (Udaipur: Himanshu Publications, 1992), p. 169–70.
5. K.K. Jacob, "Social Development Perspectives and Trends in India", in *Contemporary Social Work,* Vol. XII (Lucknow: Deptt. of Social Work April, 1995), p. 20.
6. V.D. Mehta, "Curriculum for Social Development", Jacob (ed.) *Social Development Perspective*. p. 182.
7. Surendra Singh, "Community Organisation", S. Singh & K.S. Soodans, *Horizons of Social Work* (Lucknow: Jyotsana Publication, 1986), p. 106.
8. R.R. Singh, "Social Work and Social Action: Some Reflections" in H.Y. Siddiqui's *Social Work and Social Action* (New Delhi: Harnam Publication, 1984), p. 87.
9. *Ibid.*
10. Statham quoted by R.R. Singh, in "Social Work and Social Action: Some Reflections", in H.Y. Siddiqui's *Social Work and Social Action.* p. 88.
11. *Ibid* p. 89.
12. J.P. Narayan quoted by R.R. Singh, in "Social Work & Social Action: Some Reflections", in H.Y. Siddiqui's *Social Work & Social Action.*
13. Warren Christopher quoted by Mirza R. Ahmed, "Emerging Trends in Social Work", in S. Singh & K.S. Soodan *Horizon of Social Work,* p. 179.
14. Sethi quoted by Mirza R. Ahmed, "Social Development & Human Rights", in *Journal of Social Work* (Lucknow: Deptt. of Social Work, 1991), p. 4.
15. Iyer quoted by Mirza R. Ahmed, "Emerging Trends in Social Work", in Singh & Soodan, *Horizons of Social Work,* p. 182.
16. S.H. Pathak *Social Welfare,* p. 130.

CHAPTER III

MANAGING THE FALLOUT OF DEVELOPMENT IN INDIA

The term 'social development' is now a part of our vocabulary but still it needs to be redefined in the present context. The definition given by ASSWI President to the University of Sheffield, U.K. is quite relevant for this purpose. "Social development is a process of systematic change (values, attitudes, institutions and practices) purposefully initiated through the instruments of social policy and planning for the enrichment of the levels of living and quality of life of the mass of people especially the weaker section, in an eco-friendly, socially just and participatory environment."[1] In this definition the concept of 'systematic change' is taken up as the central theme of social development. There cannot be any controversy regarding its importance in the context of development. However, the problems regarding the philosophy of social development start when the conflict between economic and social aspects of development emerges. The economists of 70s were not ignorant about the importance of social development. Well known economist V.K.R.V. Rao explains that "the essential elements of development are not only economic but also social, ethical, political and psychological and the end product arrived at, is a better and more fulfilled human being."[2] The economist Benjamin Higgins expressed similar views in 1963 saying "Expenditure on education, health, housing and the like are not merely means to economic development. They ARE economic development."[3]

This shows that even economist were convinced about the role played by social factors in development.

Side Effects of Developmental Programmes

No doubt, people started understanding the importance of non material factors. One more point is obvious by the above discussion that economic development is closely linked with social development. Economic development without social development is not much meaningful. But sometimes economic growth appears appreciable and desirable for a while in underdeveloped countries even without social development. However, in the long run, economic development without social development creates problems. This fact was known much earlier. Mahatma Gandhi and his disciples have written right from the beginning about hazardous growth of social and economic forces in the society. Mahatma Gandhi writes at one place "The craze is what they call labour saving machinery. Men go on saving labour till thousands are without work and thrown on the open street to die of starvation. I want to save time and labour not for a fraction of mankind but for all .... today machinery merely helps a few to ride on the back of millions."[4] This may be only partially true but there is no doubt that the side effects of development are quite complicated. The problems associated with development may be divided into three categories:

1. *Problems of General Nature*

These are simple and common type of problems. Once the traditional system of society is broken apart, there has to be a reaction. Any change or progress may create temporary mismanagement, maladjustment and cultural lag. Generation gap, youth unrest and breakdown of joint family are some examples of these types of problems which are by and large absorbed by the society because every society has a tolerance level upto certain extent. Usually these general problems are managed by the victims themselves or by the system, without outside help.

2. *Problems Associated with the Faulty Nature of Development*

Most of the time when we take up the problems concerning development we remember the bottlenecks of faulty development because they are massive and grave. The example of green revolution may be taken up; we know that before *Chakabandi* every field used to have good and solid boundaries but now those boundaries are weak. Even small rain causes a flood. The government had prepared drain system for slowing down rain water and later on using it for irrigation but most of the farmers have filled these drains and have used that area for paddy cultivation in Punjab. As a result water table has gone down which is very dangerous but farmers and consumers are only interested in the production of the best quality of rice today and nobody cares for tommorrow.

Another example might be the incident of March 15, 1966 when the then Director of Central Rice Research Institute — Cuttack, Dr. H.R. Richaria informed the Director of ICAR, against the introduction of highly disease prone rice varieties in the country. The warning was ignored completely but thirteen years later Dr. Richaria was called back to suggest ways to control rice vulnerability because so many problems have followed such as introduction of very strong pesticides.[5]

Breakdown of the family, loneliness and extremity of individualism are some common after-effects of development. They encourage alcoholism and drug addiction. According to one estimate in USA, consumers' expenditure on narcotics is believed to exceed the combined GDPs of more than 80 developing countries.[6]

These are some of the examples of faulty type of development. They make us feel that development creates poverty and misery. The income per capita in India has almost doubled within ten years (Rs. 1630 in 1980-81 to Rs. 2227 in 1990-91). But 50% of this increase goes to top 20% population and bottom 20% population only gets 7% increase.[7] No doubt the side effects of faulty development are, sometimes, quite harmful.

3. *Problems Associated with the Well Meaning Development*

Inspite of an appropriate and well-planned development some problems do creep in. For example in tribal and hilly areas roads are constructed to facilitate the lives of the tribals, but the consequences are different, because contractors now reach there easily to cut the forests and tourists and other people visit there to give sexually transmitted diseases (STD) to their girls.

Another example is given by HDR "During past five decades world income increased seven fold (in real GDP) and income per person more than triple (in per capita GDP) but this growth has been highly unequal. Between 1960 and 1991 the share of the world's income for richest 20% of the global population rose from 70% to 85% while the share of the poorest 20% declined from 2.3% to 1.4%."[8]

The above discussion indicates that GNP oriented narrow type of development which is closer to economic growth, creates deep rooted problems. Sethi points out that, "there is long term inverse relationship between economic growth and absolute poverty." Another advocate of careful and controlled economic and social development Sugatha Dasgupta says "....development and welfare have been responsible for creation of absolute poverty .... Development has been responsible for much of the misery."[9]

If this is true than what should be done? Should there be no development? Or should there be some precautions in planning for development? A careful and planned development will provide answer for this. Development which is not for today; development which does not push poverty and deprivation into future and development which is not temporary and momentary, that should be the development in the real sense. In other words we should have 'sustainable development.'

Sustainable Development — Concept & Philosophy

So much development and growth have taken place but the process of development in India is now creating a situation which human beings and environment can not take any more though the life expectancy has increased, production has multiplied, yet in absolute number we are having more hungry, illiterate and deprived people. Safe drinking water is still a dream in India; the gap between rich and poor is widening. John Lupien from FAO points out: That the number of chronically under-nourished in Africa had grown from 101 million to 168 million in the past two decades. Nearly 13 million children die every year. 2000 million people suffer from lack of vital micro-nutrients ....[10]

In India the situation is not so grim but we are heading towards worse days; however one thing is clear that development has not given any relief to the poor population.

In 1983 World Commission on Environment and Development was established by U.N. General Assembly. It organised deliberations and discussion forums. The findings were alarming such as: Development makes people poor and vulnerable and the environment is badly exploited for development. Some measures which were suggested for improvement, were as follows:

1. Human needs should be controlled.
2. Poverty eradication programmes should be given the utmost priority.
3. All development programmes should be eco-friendly.

This was an early conscious effort towards sustainable development. Later HDR 1994 gives a definition to sustainable development. "Sustainable human development puts people at the centre of development and points out forcefully that the inequalities of today are so great that to sustain the present form of development is to perpetuate similar inequalities for future generation. The essence of sustainable development is that, everyone should have equal access to development opportunities now and in future."[11] To clarify the point further one may add that development should stop dwindling with acute problems like poverty and deprivation and do something meaningful to eradicate them as far as possible in an ecofriendly manner.

To have sustainable development, equality and equitable distribution of resources, not only between human beings but also among the rich and the poor nations is necessary. It is global equality which ultimately leads to sustainable development. HDR remarks over this point "the life style of the rich nations will clearly have to change, the North America and Western Europe has roughly one-fifth of the World's population and four-fifth of its income. It consumes 70% of the world's energy, 75 per cent of its metals and 85% of its wood. If the eco-sphere were fully priced not free, then such consumption pattern could not continue.

"A major restructuring of the world's income distribution, production and consumption pattern may therefore be a necessary precondition for any viable strategy for sustainable human development."[14] When this definition is examined in Indian context, it is easy to understand that 'political will' is as important as social will.

A careful study of developed countries and their models of development, reveals some less known aspects which alarm the developing countries, and some times, they should try to keep away from the model followed by the developed countries. Some of the findings about the developed countries' socio-economic situation are quite unbelievable. According to HDR 1991, 13 per cent people of USA are poor and near about 11 million are near poverty line. In developed countries income is higher, even then indicators of development such as education have become a mockery, people are not getting higher education. Adults who have dropped upper secondary constitute, 78 per cent in Spain, 72 per cent in Italy, 57 per cent in Belgium and 49 per cent in France. 25 million adults in USA could not read or understand a warning on the bottle of medicines, 14 per cent adults could not locate their country on the world map and 75 per cent adults could not place Persian Gulf on it.[15]

Scientific advancement of this computer age creates behavioural problems such as marketing pornography in the form of digitized images. A study titled 'Marketing Pornography on the Information Super Highway' (Mellow University Pennsylvania) explains some facts. They found out that on network, 83.5 per cent pictures were pornographic which were used as time passing games.[16] Not only this, increase in diseases like cancer, road accidents, suicides, rapes and crimes indicate pathological trends. This is ironical that people in developed countries are well aware of all these facts, even then sufficient and honest efforts have not been made to streamline developmental strategies in the developed countries. Right now we feel that even scientists have joined the race of money making. They are working in arms and heroin manufacturing underground factories without any sense of shame and guilt.

The World Commission on Environment & Development (Brundtland Report) puts this point very strongly by explaining that at least half a million scientists are working for weapon researches, i.e. military research and arms development research. Developing world is spending much more amount than what is being spent on energy sources, health, agriculture and population control.

This is quite obvious that development without precautions can be more harmful than the situation of 'no development.'

Pre-requisite for Sustainable Development

There are certain pre-conditions for planning a development strategy so that it should not bring poverty and deprivation in future. The development should take the society towards a long-term improvement and well-being. Some of these pre-conditions are:

1. An International distribution system based on justice and equality between developed and developing countries.
2. Prosperity and production, but not at the cost of ecological balance.
3. A social system which cares for the poor and down-trodden, which also promotes all the sections of the society and does not create unnecessary rift among them.
4. A technology, which is not based on the unmindful imitation of the foreign technology.
5. An economic system, which is not selfish, greedy or short sighted.
6. A political system, which is based on democracy and welfare state principles.
7. An education system, which is utilitarian and academic both.

8. A government which is free from corruption and enjoys people's trust.
9. A strong family system, where individual freedom is also appreciated to a great extent.

If these pre-conditions exist then sustainable development would flourish. It is not all the time possible to have all the conditions in the proper form, but whatever is possible, should be achieved.

Salient Features of Sustainable Development

There is no doubt that prosperity and wealth are required for planning and implementing social service, welfare or development. Inspite of that we have to be careful about GNP based narrow concept of development. It is a meaningless pursuit as an economist remarks: "A country that cut down all its trees, sold them as wood chips and gamble the money away playing tiddly, winks, would appear from its national accounts to have got richer in terms of GNP per person." It is needless to say that this is a momentary and disguised development. A long lasting development would "include needs such as water, food, nutrition, clothing, shelter, recreation, minimum norm of education and medical facilities. This, even if the GNP is going up and there is a deterioration at the lowest levels in meeting the basic needs of people, then the desirability of this development pattern can be seriously questioned."[17]

Keeping the above discussion in view here are some measures which will make social-development a sustainable development instead of momentary or harmful type of growth.

In sustainable and long lasting development strategies, globalisation of welfare and development should be the first step because it is not important to have fair economic system or social justice within a country only, but it should be practised at the international level also. The whole world is a village and if one section is deprived then sooner or later the other sections are also going to suffer. HDR brought out by United Nations mentions, "The concept of sustainability is greatly endangered in a world that is one-fourth rich and three-fourth poor, that is half democratic and half authoritarian, where poor nations are being denied equal access to global economic opportunities, where the income disparity between the richest 20 percent and the poorest 20 percent of the world has doubled over the past three decades, where one fourth of the humanity is unable to meet its basic needs and where, such nations are, consuming four-fifth of humanity's natural capital without being obliged to pay for it."[18] At this point one is made to think of certain issues. Is global planning possible? How any policy's implementation is possible in the whole world? As a matter of fact, it should be a task for developed countries because they are the powers who matter. UN bodies can take initiative but they are also under the influence of developed western world. As a result it is possible only when they will make sacrifices for globalizing welfare and development. Any effort of equitable distribution of resources will make them somewhat deprived therefore their willingness is more crucial.

Another point of concern is the problem of wasteful consumption. Production of ice-creams, chocolates and fancy cakes adds something into wasteful consumption. This is ironical that many people in our country are not getting even drinking water. Production of these fancy goods is meant only for high class or upper middle class people. Dogra remarks quoting Chossudovsky "... in most of the third world countries approximately 60 per cent of national income is concentrated in the upper 20 per cent of the population. In many low and middle income developing countries, 70 per cent of the rural households have a per capita income which is between 10 and 20 per cent of that national average".[19] In this connection two questions may be asked.

a) Should the production of fancy consumable items be stopped?
b) If it is stopped, is it possible to spend the saved money on essential goods which should be provided on subsidised rates for deprived masses?

In a democratic society, characterized by liberalized economy, people are free to produce and purchase whatever they want but government must take initiative to produce essential goods for more needy and deprived people. Besides, fixing up production priorities, more effective steps should be taken for eradication of poverty for providing more purchasing power to a common man.

One more feature of sustainable development is low cost or cost effectiveness of the planned projects. People's involvement, their participation, empowerment and ultimately their leadership bring all the programmes nearer to the beneficiaries. Development will be really sustainable when it will not be considered a government programme. It will be sustained as people's programme.

Next feature of sustainable development is family planning, birth control and an effective population policy which makes human beings economically and socially productive units and not burdens. Planning population growth is basically a matter of equality of life and investment on human beings. More investment in human beings will definitely lead to a careful 'production' of human beings.

If the world's population would continue growing with the same speed then all developmental strategies will be futile and sustainable development will be just a chimera.

One more feature for sustainable development is environmental protection. Global warming, green house effect, depletion of the ozone layer, deforestation, drought, famine, floods and earthquakes are caused by ruthless exploitation of nature and the natural wealth. Environmental exploitation has far reaching effects. It has been mentioned at one place: "The considerations of social justice and environment protection now clearly point in the same direction [we should] give up the obsession with growth, try to curtail all wasteful and frivolous productions as much as possible, concentrate on meeting the basic needs of all people, redistribute the wealth and income on a significant scale at the international level and within nations."[20] Here it is worth mentioning that in the field of environment protection 'ecofeminism' is another growing philosophy. Vandana Shiva a great supporter of eco-feminism points out "…. a gender based ideology remains totally inadequate in either responding to the ecological crisis, created by patriarchal and violent modes of relating to nature, or in understanding how third world women are leading ecological struggles based on values of conservation which are immediately generalised as the concern for entire communities and regions and even humanity as a whole."[21] Here the role of women in maintaining ecological balance is emphasised because most of the destruction is caused by men. Her role in protecting ecological balance should be supported and promoted because protecting environment ultimately means sustainability of the developmental measures.

One more salient feature for sustainable development is the preservation of human rights. Nanavatty explains in one of his papers that there is deep relationship between social development and human right.[22] These rights, for developed and developing countries may not be different but their practical applicability is different. Some important rights are still far off dreams such as right to the disabled because only 1 per cent disableds receive meaningful services in the whole world (HDR 1994),[23] right to equality to women, who are ill paid, victims of female circumcisions, forced to work as prostitutes and suffering due to family and social violence and right to education for a child who is perhaps forced to work as child labour (330 million children all over the world are missing their school for vocation). There is a long list of these rights which are not given to people in the real sense at least in the under developed Asian and African countries. In the list of all these rights one more right may be added; Ahmed describes it: United Nations and other international agencies, have, thus, promoted the concept of 'the right to development' which means everyone's right to participate in the process of development and to have a fair share of its benefits.[24] In Indian context inspite of the recognition to the importance of human rights, sometimes we see violation of all human rights to a great extent. One tends to remember the policy of appeasement just before Second World War when all the world powers including League of Nations were tolerating German aggressions because they imagined that ultimately that would go against (former) USSR. In the same way we ignore violation of human rights because it is not hurting 'us' but it may destroy our enemies. This is important to note that no sustainable development is possible without assuring human rights to all the citizens in the country. Not only this, violation of human rights in other countries also retards the process of social justice in one's own country.

Another essential feature is the provision of all the essential goods and services for all the fellow beings for controlled and reasonable consumption. This does not mean high level production of luxury goods because high level production, sometimes co-exists with poverty. More production may also harm environment, therefore, reasonable production and fair distribution is more important than more production and haphazard distribution. Sustainable development is for today, tommorrow and day after tommorrow. Therefore, it must support water, soil, trees, animals and humans because they can only survive when they are together.

An important feature of sustainable development is the use of scientific discoveries for reducing utilisation of natural resources. e.g. development of CFC free fridges and intelligent building. CFC free fridges protect ozone layer and sensitive buildings 'decide' with the help of computer and other equipment how to use air and natural light and economize electricity and other resources. (In Delhi I.F.C.'s Central Office, American Express, World Bank, SCOPE and HABITAT are sensitive buildings). These buildings are more secure and fire proof also. Sustainable development does not mean that we should ignore scientific progress and insist only on traditional technology. As a matter of fact it is science which has created awareness regarding global warming, green house effect, acid rains and harmful effects of deforestation.

Social Development and Sustainable Development

It has been discussed at length that economic development with out social development creates deprivation in the long run. The term social development is traditionally used for not only more production but also for fair distribution. The above mentioned salient features of sustainable development also highlight the importance of social justice, global justice, equity and equitable distribution of resources. Now the question arises as to how are the two types of development different? If they are not different then, are they identical?

In fact these two approaches and programmes are not identical but definitely they have a deep relationship. In nutshell they can be taken as 'cause and effect' of each other. Sustainable development creates social development and social development eventually nurtures futuristic attitude among masses. Then they feel the need of 'sustaining' development. They do not live for today, they rather plan a long term strategy.

We can also take sustainable development as a more advanced approach in comparison to social development because:

— Social development is usually concerned with human beings but sustainable development is thoughtful and careful for all species, eco-system and the whole biosphere because human existence depends on the existence of other creatures in the natural surrounding.

— Sustainable development is more futuristic in comparison to social development because it believes in the postponement of consumption so that the coming generations should not suffer from deprivation. Social development is primarily concerned with the rise in the standard of living of the down trodden masses whereas sustainable development promotes austerity, simplicity and low consumerism.

— Sustainable development cares a lot for indigenous people, folk culture and primitive technology. It is felt that least interference policy, for the primitive people, should be adopted because western technology, some times, proves to be very harmful. However, it does not mean that scientific inventions and discoveries should not be promoted. In fact new discoveries can help in economizing natural resources. Sustainable development philosophy appreciates a purposeful use of scientific advancement and disapproves of the use of science for greed and power.

It is needless to say, that there are so many common features between social development and sustainable development. No doubt they are complimentary to each other.

However, now it is quite clear that development may be sustained only when harmony is created between human beings and environment. They are interdependent. If their interdependence is disturbed then the consequences may be quite serious. In the name of development natural resources are destroyed. So much harm has already been done. Now we should not tolerate these harmful effects as normal side effects of development. They should be managed with the help of sustainable development strategies.

NOTES

1. ASSWI *News Letter* Nagpur, 1994, M.S.S. Institute of Social Work, Vol. 1, No. 2.
2. V.K.R.V. Rao, *Values and Economic Development* (Delhi: Vikas Publication, 1971), p. 47.
3. Benjamin Higgin An Economist's Views in Part-II of UNESCO, *Social Aspect of Economic Development in Latin America* (Paris: 1963), p. 185.
4. Gandhi, *Young India,* 13 November, 1924 p. 85-86.
5. Bharat Dogra, *Encyclopedia of Development Environment & Welfare* (New Delhi: 1995), p. 103.
6. *Human Development Report*, 1994.
7. Sunder Lal Bahuguna, "Development Redefined", *The Indian Journal of Public Administration*, July–Sept. 1993 (Vol. XXXIX, Nos. 3), p. 232.
8. *HDR* 1994.
9. Sugata Dasgupta, *Towards A Post Development Era* (Delhi: Mittal Publications, 1985), p. 20.
10. FAO, *Fighting Hunger* (1993).
11. *HDR* 1994.
12. J.D. Sethi, 'Poverty in India' *Azad Academy Journal*, July 1–31, 1990.
13. *HDR* 1994.
14. HDR quoted by Bharat Dogra, in *Encyclopaedia of Development Environment & Welfare*, p. 32.
15. *HDR* 1991.
16. HDR quoted by Dogra, *Encyclopaedia of Development Environment & Welfare*, p. 11.
17. Dogra, *Encyclopaedia of Development Environment & Welfare*, p. 24.
18. *HDR* 1994.

19. Bharat Dogra, *Encyclopaedia of Development Environment & Welfare*, p. 49.
20. *Ibid* p. 20.
21. Vandana Shiva *Staying Alive* (New Delhi: Kali for Women 1992), p. 54.
22. M.C. Nanavarthi, 'Impact of Globalization of Market Economy on Social Development & Human Right', paper presented in Asian and Pacific Association of Social Work Education Conference held from 17-20 Nov. 1993 at Tata Institute of Social Sciences, Bombay.
23. *HDR* 1994.
24. Mirza Ahmed, "Social Development & Human Rights" in *Journal of Social Work* Vol. VIII (Lucknow, Deptt. of Social Work 1991). p. 6–7.

CHAPTER IV

STRATEGIZING SUSTAINABLE DEVELOPMENT

In June 1972, the First Earth Summit, the U.N. Conference on the Environment was held in Stockholm — Sweden. Exactly 20 years later in June 1992 — the Second Earth Summit was held in Rio de Janerio — Brazil in which two treaties were signed, one for minimizing global warming and the other for protecting biodiversity. People in the summit felt that the whole planet has seen maddening growth of pollution, population and pressure. Not only that, within these twenty years we could also understand the adverse relationship between ruthless development and ecological disaster. As a result gradual and carefully planned eco-friendly development was designed. This eco-friendly development was called 'sustainable development'. In 1987 Brundtland Commission on Environment & Development presented its report titled "Our Common Future". It emphasized on sustainability of the developmental activities. The report defines sustainable development in these words: "In order for development to be sustainable, it must meet the needs of the present without compromising the ability of future generations to meet their own needs".[1] No doubt this is rather a too general definition but this is what is commonly understood by sustainable development. From the point of view of developed countries it is a question of managing environmental crisis which is due to over consumerism, and from the developing countries angle it is nothing of the sort. They feel that poverty is working as polluter and with prosperity this problem will be managed. They also feel that exploitation of natural resources is also due to poverty, over-population and ignorance. Once these problems are controlled, exploitation of nature will also come down.

Components of Sustainable Development

Indian and western approaches regarding sustainable development would be discussed later in this chapter. Before that we should be clear about the focus and components of sustainable development. They are:

1. Survival and continuation of the humans on earth.
2. Maintenance of basic ecological processes.
3. Control overpopulation growth.
4. Provision of basic material needs of all humans.
5. Satisfaction of non material needs of all humans.
6. Little use of non-renewable resources.
7. Reduction of harmful waste and its production.
8. Increased reliance on sustainable and renewable resources.
9. Restricted and planned consumption.
10. Global redistribution of the means of production.
11. Increased consumption of essential goods in developing countries.
12. Restricted production of superfluous goods.
13. Minimum resource use and waste production.[2]

R.P. Mishra also discussed some objectives, he particularly emphasised on equity and justice. He feels that equity and justice are the synonymous of sustainable development. He divided them into four dimensions (1) equity among nations — rich nations, poor nations and developed nations and developing nations. (2) equity between regions, classes and gender etc. (3) equity between generations (present and future) (4) equity between economics and ecology and science and spirituality.[3]

It is obvious that sustainable development is a large scale participatory activity. It is not a job of the government or higher authorities only. It is very much a concern of each and everyone. Some can contribute directly, some indirectly.

It involves planners, government officials. Industrialists, teachers, housewives, tribals, manufactures, students, shop-keepers, scavengers, rag pickers, in short every one. It should proliferate like mass movement. It is massive and vast. Mishra remarks, "Sustainable development can be looked at, from a variety of perspectives, such as environmental, economic, social, political, cultural and technological. None of the perspectives can stand alone. Sustainable development is possible if all of them are taken into consideration."[4]

Today the stark questions are: How can we save our planet ? How can we develop without depleting environment and social system? How can we salvage the planet from the damage which has already been caused ? and, what should be the strategies for future ? All these questions are inter-connected. The problem of survival of the earth is too serious to be dealt with small and sporadic efforts. Mourice F. Strong (who became the Secretary General of the UNCED in 1992) said in 1989, "we have been literally living off the Earth's capital and that capital is being seriously depleted. We can not continue to run our planet this way and more than we could run a business for long by running down and living off its capital. Indeed our Earth if it were an incorporated entity, would be headed for bankruptcy if we continue on our present course."[5] Here one should not forget the Indian view point. Typical Indian concept of co-existence with the nature is based on the simplification and 'no industrialisation' approach which has been discussed at length by Mahatma Gandhi, Vinobha Bhave, Sunder Lal Bahuguna, Sugata Dasgupta and later on by Vandana Shiva etc.

Strategies for Sustainable Development

With the above discussion this has been established that both developing as well as developed nations are getting more and more involved in the problem of environment preservation, but this is rather surprising to note that the strategies for solving this problem are quite different in India and the West. By and large Indian philosophy promotes environment preservation whereas the western views are in favour of reconstructing and repairing the damaged environment.

They do not go for reducing their level of consumption or standard of living, but they have certainly decided to reduce pollution and wasteful use of natural resources. Some examples of the same are discussed by James Gustane Speth such as:

1. *Energy efficiency* : Inventors are manufacturing the family cars in such a way which will provide more average and building the houses with new superinsulated material that requires just 1/10 of the present energy consumption for heating. New gas turbines cogenerate electricity and heat 50 percent more effectively than today's power plants.
2. *Renewable energy and biotechnology* : With the help of biotechnology a plan was prepared for solar electricity. Besides that wind biomass are developing as other renewable sources of energy. It is estimated that solar energy industry will overshadow all other types of power production in the early next century. More over new microbial and bioengineered product can work as pesticides to promote agriculture.
3. *Waste minimization* : 'No Waste' technology can be developed due to improved manufacturing techniques. This will control gaseous sludge and liquid waste both in volume and toxcity.
4. *New communication system* : Above all this, satellite remotesensing, monitoring instrumentation, artificial intelligence for environment management and educational programming will be developed and widely used with the help of computer and telecommunication techniques. This will save environment to a great extent. Computer aided designs and systems will reduce the wastage of the raw material and natural resources.[6]

Analysis of the Issue

With the above discussion it is clear that developed western countries have prepared definite plans of action to look after the environment. Moreover they are in a position to take certain actions which their aware and conscious public will religiously follow. For example not letting any factory be established unless it is totally approved of by the environmentalist, checking new technologies thoroughly because the harmful effects may appear after a decade or so, controlling the production or use of polythene and stopping the preparation of CFCs etc. But India and most of the other Afro-Asian countries are not at this stage. Their public is not so much involved in the environmental issues, moreover their haphazard industrialization and population explosion is creating environmental hazards inspite of their low level of consumption. In India, somehow, the approach to development and environment is different. This is an approach of least disturbance to natural balance in the ecological system by minimum possible exploitation to nature. Mahatma Gandhi, his disciples and modern environmentalists all have felt that not much of disturbance is required if there is no over consumption. No doubt, environment needs maintenance and even in the name of development, environmental exploitation can not be justified. Vandana Shiva writes, "The assumptions are evident; nature is unproductive; organic agriculture based on nature's cycle of renewability spells poverty; women and tribals and peasant societies embedded in nature are similarly unproductive, not because it has been demonstrated that in co-operation they produce less goods and services for needs, but because it is assumed that production takes place only when mediated by technologies for commodity production, even when such technologies destroy life. Stable and clean river is not a productive resource in this view: it needs to be 'developed' with dams in order to become so .... Natural forest remain unproductive till they are developed into monoculture plantation of commercial species."[7]

This ironical description has given an understanding that according to modern thinking untouched nature is not sufficient for needs, it should be tailored according to commercial need, though this process may destroy bio-diversity of a particular area. Basically, every small change in the life support system has far reaching effects. But it is possible that its effects are discernible after decades.

Indian thinkers and environmentalists are concerned about cultural and biological diversity. Sustainable development is not possible without it. The earth is shared by 30 million life forms such as plants, microbes and animals but every day possibly 1 to 25 species are doomed to extinction, never to be reborn. It is all due to human hands and in the name of human development. Sunder Lal Bahuguna rightly feels that nature (Prakriti) has perverted (Vikriti) and destroys lives due to floods and droughts as it is disrupted and thwarted.[8]

When we think of justice and equality we should not ignore the share of other species. It is not only a moral stand but also a selfish need because our existence depends on the existence of others. As Ashish Kothari writes, "If as a specie we are truly attempting to live peacefully and wisely, then we will have to learn to respect life and diversity much more than we have in the last couple of hundred years. Biological and cultural diversity must become the keystones of our endeavour. As such after fulfilling the basic human material needs of food, water and air we must ask ourselves: What more can we obtain for ourselves without violating the rights of other human and non-human creatures? And if we get an answer that our material desires are impinging on the rights of other human beings and other creatures, then it is time to call a halt to the process of economic growth."[9]

It is worth mentioning that at conceptual level Indian Philosophy is in favour of sustaining ecological balance but as far as practice is concerned an average Indian is basically indifferent towards any type of eco-friendly activities. A poor villager is worried about his two square meals, unguided youths are following gun culture, not realising that terrorism is also ruining the environment, ruthless cutting of trees in Kashmir by militants for maintaining self-styled army of rebels, polluting water and atmosphere by using hand made raw arms and ammunition, are examples, to mention a few. A middle class housewife is putting a candle and flower in the holy rivers after every worship. In other words everyone is participating in the process of environment destruction.

Businessmen, politicians and people at the top are creating ecological problems due to GATT and globalisation. This new inequality and injustice is being forced on the Third World through the patent system and intellectual property right by GATT, the World Bank and the US Trade Act. The new North South asymmetries will generate an unstable world and are ofcourse an issue of major concern. Equally serious is the underming of the sovereignty of the Third World."[10]

Contemporary Indian Scenario

Indian history, culture and psyche believe in the concept of co-existence. The importance of forest in our tradition, worship of rivers, incarnation of gods in the form of animals etc. are the proofs of one fact that the primitive man knew the eternal relationship in which whole universe is bound. But unconsciously the present generation has cut down its relationship with that traditions, rather it takes nature as a slave. In Indian context some strategies should be developed keeping in view our specific needs. Some of these possible strategies are given below:

1. It is not enough to believe that traditional Hindu Philosophy is eco-friendly because Hindu gods took birth in the form of plants and animals. We have to see very carefully whether our beliefs and practices are really eco-friendly or not. Let us take the example of making snakes drink milk and harming its metabolism or worshiping the trees like *Peepal* but never planting it deliberately. It is evident that eco-friendly behaviour will have to be defined and learnt with efforts.
2. In many cases, initial disturbance of a bio-diverse atmosphere and after that an effort to reconstruct it, is a wrong approach because once disturbed eco-system can not be reconstructed so easily, for example once destroyed rain forests do not grow, easily rather deciduous forests take their place. Once burnt forest (due to *jhoom* cultivation) do not grow on its own, rather shrubs and bushes grow in that area, once cut big mature trees' loss can not be compensated by planting a new one because an old tree is a habitat and vital part of eco-system whereas a new

plant is not a habitat of so many birds, insects and microbe. Its role is entirely different in eco-system. It means that minimum interference with the nature is the best policy. Most of the time human ways to develop nature have serious after-effects.

3. Craze of over production for business is quite harmful in the larger context because it leads to commercialization of natural products. As Vandana Shiva remarks "Diverse systems have multiple outputs and yields, and much of these outputs flow back within the system to allow for low external input production, so that production is possible without access to purchasing power, credit and capital. Livestock and crops help maintain each other's productivity symbiotically and sustainably.... Homogeneous and one dimensional production systems break up community structure, displace people from diverse occupation."[11] There is no doubt that effort to produce more and more only satisfy greed and not the need.
4. Environmentalists also feel that projects like green revolution or white revolution are not so profitable in the long run. Claude Alvares points out that heavy subsidies are required for green revolution like fertilizer subsidy was crossing 5000 crore in 1990. Moreover sometimes actual consumption of necessary goods goes down, for example availability of pulses per head per day was 64 gram in 1962 but it gradually reduced to 40 gram in 1979. More production and use of pesticides is also associated with green revolution. Not only this, the 'Sevin' manufactured for fertilizer in Union Carbide Bhopal Plant was an essential component of green revolution technology. Besides, on social front there is a displacement of tenant, marginal and small farmers by rich farmers all over.[12]
5. Population explosion is obviously very harmful and there is no need to find further proofs for it. Now the need is that those who do not follow family planning should not be taken as ignorant and innocent people, they should be treated as trouble creator. They should be condemned thoroughly in the society because they are not only harming themselves, but they are harming the whole society and the ecology also. Their act should be taken as an

anti human activity. If they are national leaders then their offence is still more severe. They are not only harming the country by various scams and scandals but also by setting wrong precedence and adding burden on country's meagre resources.

Here it would not be irrelevant to mention that United Nations Environmental Programme (UNEP) has its own priority. A workshop which was held in Madras confirms this. It was titled 'Environmental Communication & Information Strategy for 1995–2000'. Suvit Yodamini the UNEP Director writes at one place that UNE programme "aims to respond to four principal environmental challenges, namely sustainable management and use of natural resources, sustainable production and consumption, a better environment for human health and well being and globalization trends and the environment."[13] It is quite clear that these points are fundamental and interlinked. They are not new also. Sustainable development has been taken as a whole entity. These issues are not only Indian issues, they are global issues. However, they are more significant in the sub-continent.

In the final analysis we can say that some environmentalists are very well aware of the harmful effects of ruthless development but majority is indifferent because of no futuristic approach among masses, Indian masses are appreciating the commercial development. As a result forests and other natural resources are getting squeezed drastically. This temporary and hollow prosperity of today is taking us towards a bankrupt and barren tomorrow.

NOTES

1. Brundtland quoted by R.P. Mishra, "Sustainable Development": The Ecological Perspective" in *Indian Journal of Public Administration,* July–Sept. 1993, Vol. XXXIX, No. 3, p. 254.
2. Stephen Dovers, "Sustainability Definition, Clarification and Concept", in *Development* (Italy: Society for International Development, 1989), p. 34.
3. Mishra, "Sustainable Development", p. 255.
4. *Ibid.* p. 257.

5. Maurice F. Strong, "Ending Hunger through Sustainable Development", in *Development* SID 1989, p. 44.
6. James Gustave Speth 'Promising Solution' in *Development*, SID p. 32.
7. Vandana Shiva, *Staying Alive* (New Delhi: Kali for Women; 1992), p. 4.
8. Sunder Lal Bahuguna, "Development Redefined", in *The Indian Journal of Public Administration*, p. 230.
9. Ashish Kothari, "Is Sustainable Development Desirable and Possible", in *The Indian Journal of Public Administration*, p. 253.
10. Vandana Shiva, *Biodiversity the Third World Perspective* (Malaysia: A Third World Network, 1994) p. 27.
11. *Ibid* p. 12.
12. For detailed description of the facts see Claude Alvares, *Science Development & Violence* (Delhi: Oxford University Press 1992) p. 40–41.
13. *Down to Earth* (Fortnightly) (New Delhi: Centre for Science and Environment; 41 Tughlakabad Institutional Area, January 15, 1996), p. 6.

CHAPTER V

POLICY MATTERS, POLITICAL GAMES AND SUSTAINABLE DEVELOPMENT

It is noteworthy that Indian concern for environment, was for the first time manifested in 1972 with Prime Minister Mrs. Indira Gandhi's address at Stockholm in UN Conference on the Human Environment. Around that time some important legislations were passed such as Wild Life Protection Act (1972), Water Act, Prevention and Control of Pollution Act (1974). Besides, during this period Project Tiger was also initiated. In mid-seventies *Chipko* movement gained momentum and became a craze. In 1980 the Department of Environment was established in the Centre and the Forest (Conservation) Act was enacted. Here it is interesting to note that Mr. B.B. Vohra Chairman, Advisory Board of Energy, wrote "A Charter for the Land" in 1972 but no body noticed that. Ten years later in 1982, 'The State of India's environment: The first Citizen's Report" was understood and appreciated by the masses. In other words some scientists were concerned right from the beginning but not the common man.

Some Unrealistic Policies

No doubt some work was done, inspite of that, certain policies were not clear regarding basic issues. For example National Wasteland Development Board, which was established with great hopes, was wound up silently without assigning any reason for it in 1985.[1] This is not the only instance of faulty planning and policy making. Drought Prone Area Programme (DPAP) is another example of the same mismanagement. It was started once in 1970-71 in (54+18) 72 districts but it was made eco-friendly only after a few years. Even then, it was not so successful because ".... meagre resources have been provided resulting in their spread over areas. During Sixth and Seventh Plans, for example, the outlay per block was Rs. 1.5 lakh per year only. Lack of integrated approach has been another deficiency. Besides, inadequate attention has been paid to maintenance."[2]

Another policy confusion arises due to Forest Conservation Act (1962) and the National Wasteland Development Board policies. M.N. Buch describes some of his experiences "The closed forest are also required to meet *nistar* requirement .... the ban of felling has also resulted in stoppage of all silvicultural operations .... a density over 0.7. . . has eliminated the other species which were naturally adapt under a mixed Chir Forest .... the dense canopy denies adequate light to seedling."[3] The policy should be against commercial felling but human dependence on forest in a restricted manner as it is in the natural atmosphere should not have been stopped. Moreover overlapping of wasteland and reserved forest land is also a common confusion. This confusion has damaged the whole programme. The policy of forest conservation is rather sporadic. Over activity of the industries based on forest wealth has been overlooked. For example it has been sensed by B.B. Vohra that saw mills are working in Himalayan belts and western ghat over time. Perhaps there is no political will to stop the continuous destruction of the thick forests.[4]

National Remote Sensing Agency and Forest Survey Department reported in 1983 that the forest cover has increased from 14.1% of the total geographical area to 19.52%. It means it has become 64.20 million hactares as against 46.35 million hectares. But when the details are studied we find that the figure was earlier like this:

36.02 m.h. — closed forest with a crown cover of 30 p.c.
10.06 m.h. — open forest with crown cover between 10–30 p.c.
00.27 m.h. — mangroves

The revised figure is described like this:

35.77 m.h. — closed forest with a crown cover of 40 p.c.
27.66 m.h. — open forest with a crown cover between 10–40 p.c.
00.77 m.h. — mangroves and coffee plantation.[5]

This increase is due to the inclusion of marginal forest area within the definition of open forests.

It shows that the closed forest are reducing and open forests are increasing which means real thick (rain) forest are vanishing and thin forests are emerging which is disastrous.

We see that the present political interests are ignoring environment altogether. In the election manifesto of any party in 1996, there is no promise of ecology and environment preservation. It has already been discussed in the previous chapters that priorities regarding environment preservation are different in East and West. But one thing is common that every where it is not simply an ecological issue, rather it is more of a political issue. Walter A. Rosenbaun writes at one place in 'Environmental Politics and Policy' "The Reagan Administration refused to concede that these issues merited more than further study and resisted environmentalist pressure to propose new federal programmes to combat these dangers. By the late 1980s, however, the Bush administration seemed prepared to accept the reality of these issues and to propose new federal initiative dealing with each problem."[6]

Further, he writes about the key issues. He feels that global warming (or green house effect due to the production of carbon dioxide) acid precipitation or acid rain (due to the harmful chemical content in water vapour) and atmosphericozone depletion are the crucial concern of politicians and scientists in the west. A social work student in India knows, no doubt these are common global issues even then in Indian context, important environmental threats are a little different. Flood, famine, soil erosion, deforestation, polluted drinking water, reduction of under ground water, garbage and waste disposal and extinction of wild life are some more important issues. It does not mean that the western ecological problems are not Indian problems. As a matter of fact all these problems are interrelated. The most dangerous problem is perhaps depletion of ozone layer for which the culprits are C.F.C.s. In fact chlorofluoro carbons and halons are used everywhere for air conditioning and refrigeration. Halons are used for fire extinguishers. Once they are released they slowly go to ozone layer (say in five years) and continue to harm it for a century. Old type of fridges are producing C.F.C.s. more than others. Rosenbaum has written about areas which are having dangerously thin ozone layer. This includes many areas of American continents.[7] He writes about the people's concern. Most public opinion analyst would agree that environmentalism has become part of "the American consensus and idea deeply fixed in the firmament of values that define America's basic political beliefs."[8]

The scenario is little different in India. People find ecology a western concept. The term ecology was coined by Earnst H. Haeckel in 1878. But traditional Indian concept of eco-friendliness was already existing. It reflected in the primitive natural life style. But with population explosion environment considerations were rapidly given up in India. Many anti-environment activities were adopted. Though the country is an agricultural country yet the situations described in Seventh Plan are as follows (1). Three fourth of the Indian farmers are small farmers owning less than two hectare (5 acres) of land. (2) These three fourth farmers can only cultivate one fourth of the total agricultural land. (4) One fourth cultivate three fourth of the land.[9] It has been experimented by Dogra that poor tribals, Harijans and villagers have access to the land only if it is not so productive. The moment it becomes productive due to irrigation, it is taken over by landlords. The poor Kol tribals have to sacrifice their land in the same way. It is an experience in Manikpur, Zila Banda.[10] This type of incidents indicate petty politics every where. When we look towards global warming issue we find a different level of politics. American Scientist said that an immediate 60 p.c. cut in emission of long lived gases would be required to stabilize atmospheric concentration. But at the same time he admits that politically this is not possible.

It at least requires 20 percent cut in carbon dioxide emission by the industrialized countries latest by the year 2020. The CFCs production and consumption was considered a grave problem during 1974–84. Later on in Vienna first convention was held in this connection in 1985. In 1987 "Montreal Protocol" had consensus to control substances that deplete the ozone layer. It is not surprising that 156 countries participated in Montreal Protocol. In 1989, 81 countries further considered this problem at Helsinki.[11] There they discussed that it is not only the problem of ultra violet rays and skin cancer, but there can be many much more serious problems like concentration of carbon and rise in the sea level. In 1991, 110 countries amended it in London and 57 countries including India signed this in Copenhagen.

On the other hand India is importing outdated hazardous chemicals from the other countries. These faulty policies and political activities are going ahead almost unchecked.

After air, water pollution is another problem. The last nail in the coffen is nothing but the projects of large dams which include Tehri, Sardar Sarovar, Narmada Sagar, Suvarnarekha, Koel Karo and Auranga. They faced opposition due to possible destruction of forest, biodiverse habitats, displacement of indigenous population and environmental fall out. Not only this the expected benefits would be going to the outsiders. An internal World Bank Memo (obtained by inter Press Services) has revealed that out of 25 Indian dams, surveyed under an on-going World Bank dam safety project, none had been designed to hold back the amount of water which it is now calculated could enter their reservoirs during heavy storms. Two of these dams could be hit by floods seven times greater than they were built to survive.[12]

There is a striking similarity between Volta Dam in Ghana, Kariba Dam in Northern and Southern Rhodesia and Narmada Sagar and Sardar Sarovar dams. Both these African dams displaced thousands of tribals and destroyed biodiverse forests. However, they have been useful for big foreign companies for preparing aluminium and copper wires.[13] In the same way in India Sardar Sarovar and Narmada Sagar jointly submerge 54106 hectares of forest and 55681 hectares of cultivable land and displace 502 villages with a population of 2,30,000 people.[14] Small peasants and tribals do not need irrigation and power. They need river and surrounding forests. Power and irrigation will be used by outsiders. It is not that we do not get lessons from the past or from the other countries' destruction but we deliberately push them under the carpet because the interest of mighty and wealthy ruling class is served by big projects.

Madhav Gadgil describes in a lecture in 1989 Society for Promotion of Wasteland Development "Those benefitting from such subsidies for instance forest based industries or citizens of Bangalore and Delhi, our political masters making policy decisions as to who will be subsidized at whose cost and the bureaucracy that administers the subsidies .... have formed an alliance, the 'iron triangle'."[15]

Here one should remember that international bodies are equally involved in the problematic 'development projects'. One example is World Bank proposal of eco-development project to save wild life in seven national parks in India. This project of green funding will make traditional dwellers dole dependent paupers. There is another significant aspect also. As it is said in the editorial of Down to Earth, "How much money will be needed to implement eco-development programmes at the same scale of investment in the country's 500 odd sanctuaries? Probably Rs. 2000 crores. Do the exalted MEF bureaucrats have that kind of money. If not, then what is this anti-people experiment all about? The availability of easy foreign money has made it convenient to continue with business-as-usual — with expensive economically inappropriate and socially unjust way of doing things. In that sense foreign aid plays a very negative role."[16]

We can always see both at national and international forum that politically motivated large projects are appreciated and small, pro-people, indigenous, inexpensive and culture specific programmes are either ignored or condemned. In financing pattern of both, World Bank and the Asian Development Bank we see the same attitude, where impressive statistics and quantity overshadows. quality.

Practice Oriented Philosophy of Sustainable Development

In this way it is quite obvious that the policies of the developed countries are also faulty but Indian policies and planning has been totally ineffective and corrupt. If government and the masses are seriously thinking about social development and sustainable development then they have to plan and act with sincerity and commitment without any political bias. If we want to save our country and the whole planet then environment should be one of our priorities. Here it must be mentioned that there are certain points which should be kept in mind before developing a practice oriented philosophy of sustainable development, such as:

(1) It is neither appropriate nor desirable to develop country wise or region wise philosophy of sustainable or social development because any environment related practice will have to create either good or bad effect on the whole globe gradually. This does not mean that we should not have local or regional programmes. As a matter of fact all local programmes have far reaching effects and global programmes leave impact on small areas too. Therefore, our environment policies should be a part of an international and broader policy. This is the justification of persuading developed countries to partially share the expenditure of developing countries on sustainable development.

(2) It does not need further discussion that social justice should be the most important issue. In this connection, it should be remembered that "Environmental destruction and social injustice are often two sides of the same coin....development has succeeded only in creating small islands of affluence amidst the vast surrounding ocean of deprivation."[17] It is important that development should be accompanied by social justice programmes.

Social injustice in this context has many faces. For example the use of forest biomass for urban industries may be a great social injustice. Rusi Engineer described at an other place that some times back a mill was awarded contract for paper manufacturing and "Bamboo is supplied less than a thousandth of its market price, river and ocean water is made available totally free of cost."[18] No doubt the gap between poor and rich is going to widen much more with this type of favoritism because the rights of tribals and villagers are snatched and unmindfully given to industrialists who use them in an extremely selfish manner. Therefore, before developing any line of action, past and present policies must be examined and assessed.

(3) It is significant to note that complete withdrawal of modern techniques in industries is not possible. Therefore, we should differentiate between renewable and nonrenewable resources. Minimizing the use of non-renewable resources is a must. But over exploitation of renewable resources may also create scarcity because production and consumption speed may not tally. Keeping a check on consumerism is the beginning of sustainable development, because consumerism among rich leads to exploitation of natural resources and ultimately to deprivation among masses. But this control is the most difficult aspect of this crusade both at individual and national level. Legal and strict government measures are not enough. It is individual consciousness which is the most important factor for participating in the movement of environmont proservation and sustainable development. However, favourable attitude from the government is also a great support.

With these precautions, a philosophy and policy of sustainable development may be developed.

A future policy for sustainable development must include:

— Simple indigenous pro-people programmes.
— Discouragement to consumption of superfluous goods.
— Strategies for active participation of masses in the movement of sustainable development.
— An approach of minimum interference and not of manipulation with the nature.
— Careful assessment of green funds of international bodies provided for environmental project.
— Impartial review of power or irrigation projects which have side effects.

— Programmes for promoting social justice and population control.

In other words our policy should not be over ambitious; it should be modest one which should lead towards a gradual change.

Human Right and Sustainable Development

It is needless to say that the declaration of universal human rights by U.N. General Assembly was a ray of hope for all poor, downtrodden, victimized, marginalized and disadvantaged groups. But later on it was felt that 'development strategies can create a wider gap between haves or have nots, if the development is momentary. For sustainable development it is important to have relevant human rights to protect ecology and other aspects of sustainable development. UNO has always been concerned with the positive as well as negative effects of scientific discoveries. It is obvious that developed nations may even use scientific innovations to exploit developing nations. Therefore, in 1975, U.N. General Assembly adopted and proclaimed the declaration on the 'Use of Scientific and Technology Progress in the Interest of Peace and for the Benefit of Mankind.' One of the main principle was "All the states shall take appropriate measures to prevent the use of scientific and technological developments, particularly by state organs to limit or interfere with the enjoyments of the human rights and fundamental freedom of the individual as enshrined in the Universal Declaration of Human Rights, the International Conventions on Human Rights and other relevant International Instruments".[19]

It is surprising to note that much before the above mentioned declaration, in 1967, a charter of Algiers was adopted by the 'Ministerial Meeting of the Group of 77' assembled at Algier on 24 October 1967. They considered that spending money on environmental protection definitely clashes with their priorities of development.[20] Inspite of all these problems environmental issues were given prominence. The right to environment has been proclaimed as the first of 26 principles of the Stockholm Declaration. Due to the tussle between environment and development, U.N. Conference of

Human Environment convened a panel of 27 senior experts of environment and development in Founex. Based on their report four seminars were held in Bangkok, Addis Ababa Mexico city and Beirut. One important finding was the suggestion given to developing countries that they should "avoid as far as feasible, the mistake and distortions that have characterized the patterns of development of the industrialized societies."[21] It has suggested further that each country should take necessary steps in the light of its own cultural setup. Inspite of that there were some apprehensions. The report reads, "Unless appropriate economic action is taken there are a number of ways in which the developing countries could suffer rather than profit from the new emphasis on environment."[22] Evidently underdeveloped countries took some more time to understand their loss.

In fact, right to environment has not been clearly understood and implemented, because it is little complicated and its implementation needs lots of planning and preparation. However, one point is quite clear that the responsibility of developed countries is much more than the developing countries; not only because developed nations have more resources but also because they are the ones who are creating environmental havoc. The following figure explains it.

Deadly incursion

Production of ozone-depletors are the highest among developed countries

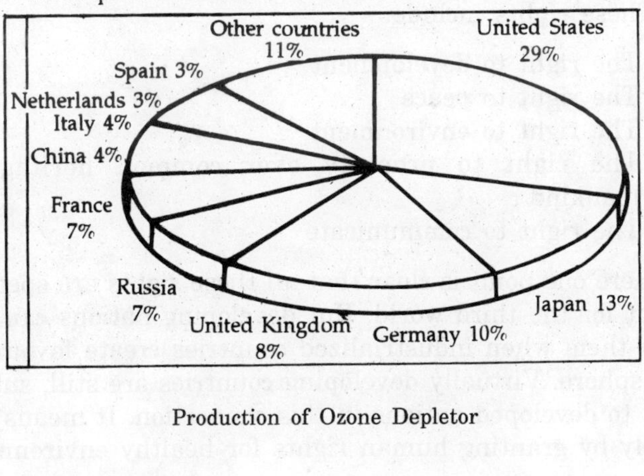

Production of Ozone Depletor

It is obvious that the main culprits are industrialized countries. However, in 10th anniversary of Vienna Convention which led to Montreal Protocol in 1987, it was decided that chloroflurocarbon (CFCs) should not be produced by developing nations after 2010 and by developed countries after 1995. It was not agreed upon by developing nations precisely because refrigeration and air conditioning in developing nations would have come to a halt. Later developing countries were allowed a breathing time till 2040 with the conditions of freezing the production at the level of 2015.[24] Does this mean that developing countries are also shying away from their responsibilities?

In this connection a little description of human rights movement would facilitate the whole discussion. There have been some landmark or turning points. As a result, Human Rights may be divided into three categories as follows:

(1) Civil and political rights (jointly called classic rights)
(2) Economic, social and cultural rights (jointly called social rights)
(3) Rights of third generation, in other words rights of developing countries (solidarity rights).[25]

According to Karel Vasak the rights of third generations/new generation/solidarity rights clearly indicate that these rights are the basic shields for the developing nations in their struggle against the particular problems faced by them in the international plane.[26]

These rights include:

(i) The right to development
(ii) The right to peace
(iii) The right to environment
(iv) The right to property over common heritage of mankind
(v) The right to communicate

Here one point is clear that all these rights are specially meant for the third world. But developing nations can only enjoy them when industrialized countries create favourable atmosphere. Virtually developing countries are still, subservient to developed nations in this connection. It means that merely by granting human rights for healthy environment, situation does not change. Developed countries have been quite vocal about their responsibilities in this field. But this is a lip service at the international platforms. In actual practices much more effort is required in this field by developed industrialized countries.

Desirable Activities and Programmes for Governments' Consideration

Governments in the countries of South East Asia (sub-continent more specifically) can experiment some programmes to save environment and bring about sustainable development. Indian sub-continent has its specific needs and limitations. Therefore some broad suggestions may be given to planners such as:

(1) Installation of tubewells should be properly planned and scrutinized, because underground water should be preserved. It is better if rain water is preserved and used for irrigation.

(2) Paper use in the government offices should be economized because trees are required in the preparation of the paper. In fact, bamboo forest have been totally depleted by West Coast Paper Mills and this destruction has extended till Andhra Pradesh, Garhwal, Assam and Nagaland.[27]

(3) Wooden furniture should not be used in the government offices. It should be replaced by bamboo or steel furniture. In the same way wood should not be used in the government buildings as far as possible. Citizens should be discouraged to use wooden furniture.

(4) Strict punishment for hunting, tree felling and polluting the environment should be introduced. All the laws should be implemented without any political favours for the rich and powerful mill owners.

(5) Policies for environment preservation should be prepared by experts and should be tested and retested before implementation.

(6) The government of our country should be very careful regarding "three core issues — enhancement of social integration (particularly of the marginalised and disad-

vantaged groups) alleviation and reduction of poverty and expansion of productive employment (and other related programmes i.e. primary health care basic education, safe drinking water, nutrition, family planning services and drug control as priority concerns) selected for the Summit are indeed important and they are also interrelated".[28]

Here it is worth mentioning that, affluent countries have started realizing their responsibility in the new issues e.g. Global Compact (20:20) which will create equality not only within but also between societies and countries. Core issues and global compact both are duties of the governments. Though people's participation is always required but governments play an important role in the above mentioned issues. It is evident that sustainable development is not just eco-friendly behaviour. Ecological balance is disturbed by poverty striken groups. Therefore core issues should be government's priority.

(7) Big projects like Narmada Sagar, Sardar Sarovar and Enron etc. should be taken up only after necessary consultation with the experts. The deciding factor should not be the income but longterm achievement for present and future generations. In case they are taken up, their profit should be shared by the local people, usually it happens that they are displaced and city dweller business men distribute the profit among themselves.

(8) Welfare projects for tribal and rural folks should not be prepared on the impressionistic basis. It often happens that the programmes are prepared but they are of no use for the beneficiaries. *Indira Awas Yojna* and National Wasteland Development Board etc. are the glaring examples of haphazard planning.

(9) Manufacturing of CFCs should be minimized because chlorofluro carbons and halons are 10,000 times more harmful than the other gases. These gases are produced mostly for fridges, air conditioners and perfumes. In many countries some other gases are experimented for refrigeration. India should also go ahead with the researches.

(10) Establishment of pharmaceuticals, plastic, polythene and

glass factories should be permitted only with all possible precautions. In case of any mishappening, responsibility should be fixed on the concerned officers. India has faced many incidents, mishappening and leakages in these type of factories.

(11) Wars, civil wars and even terrorism create all sorts of hurdles in the process of social development, sustainable development and environmental purification. Ruling and opposition political parties have major role in stopping and controlling civil wars and terrorism. Internal and external stability should be maintained and controversial issues should be resolved peacefully. Bomb explosion does not solve any problem. It creates hatred, violence and pollution. Controlling terrorism should be the priority of every government because terrorism grows due to many factors and faulty government policy is one of them. Unfortunately the developing countries are ignoring this fact and increasing their expenditure on military preparations.

(12) All projects for increased production like green revolution and white revolution should be organised carefully. Sustainability of such programmes is more important in comparison to qualitative achievements. Green revolution should be revised and should be made more eco-friendly. Long term problems associated with it should not be ignored, they should be accepted and managed as far as possible.

(13) More social justice for marginalised groups should be provided otherwise dissatisfied groups create unrest and even terror. Here it is noteworthy that programmes for providing social justice should not be based on favouritism or reservation only because they create reaction in the other groups. Long term strategies should be adopted for bringing about just distribution of the fruits of social development. It should be remembered that all short-term programmes meant for exploiting the vote banks create further complication in the long run.

(14) Government must give up the attitude of measuring social development from the point of view of economic

development and GNP per capita. Joke Schrijvers quotes Waring and says that in the process of economic development there are no calculations relating to "death, poverty, refugee population, ruined food sources, the enormous waste of investments in armaments and an increasingly fragile and exploited environment.[29]

Intellectuals have started looking beyond GNP based growth. In 1990 World Bank report on poverty was published, the United Nations Development Programme launched Human Development Index for measuring human development as an alternative to the GNP per capita. On this index U.S. slid from second to the nineteenth position in the world ladder. This shows that the earlier estimates were wrong. Schrijvers again quotes Waring and says that the nuclear submarine is equivalent to the annual education budget of 23 developing countries with 160 million school going children.[30] Government should crystalize the concept 'development', 'social development' and 'sustainable development' etc. Moreover, new indicators of social and sustainable developments should be prepared in order to have more objectivity. As per HDR, during 1991, developing countries spent four times more on defence in comparison social services like — education, population control and nutrition. If this expenditure is saved and used on social services their general standard of living will definitely improve. This will be a 'peace dividend' to these countries. It is ironical that those who are vocal about disarmament are supplying arms to developing nations and they are buying them at the cost of their basic needs.

Here one should realize that government's role is very vital in the process of sustainable development. But this does not mean that people's active participation is not required. In fact government can only initiate the process and it is for the general public to start the actual work.

Possible Strategies for Social Workers' Intervention

It has already been said that government and public must go hand in hand in the programmes of sustainable development. It is necessary that every one participates and realises his particular role in the developmental activities. Social workers and social activists are definitely required to play a significant role in this campaign. They are already participating in various capacities in this crusade. Many of them are running NGOs such as Kalpa Vriksha (Delhi), Bombay Environment Action Group (Bombay), Natural History Society (Bombay), Chhatra Yuva Sangharsh Vahini (Madhya Pradesh) and Jigyansu Tribal Research Centre (Delhi) etc. They are working in the field of environment preservation and welfare of tribal, rural and scheduled caste people. Still a lot more is required to be done. Professional social workers are lagging behind in this field to some extent. However, college of social work, Nirmala Niketan had formed Forum for Environmental Concern in 1985. Possible and desirable role of social workers and social activist may be designed on the following lines.

(1) Social workers should advocate futuristic approach. In the case of extremely poor people it is not possible but a social worker will have to create an atmosphere where investment (or conservation) for future is promoted. They will have to work at grass root level with the common man but at the same time they should participate in planning and policy making also.

(2) Social workers and social activists should promote controlled consumerist norms. Production of hazardous or at least superfluous goods (like soft drinks and potato chips etc.) should be minimized. Their consumption should be replaced by some other natural products.

(3) Professional social workers should give up the urban bias from their attitude. They should start working with rural and tribals masses. They should work for awareness generation, participation in the mainstream, wasteland development and proper utilisation of forest resources for food, fuel, fodder and fruits. Social worker's skills of establishing face to face relationship and working in the small groups should be used because people's motivation, involvement and participation are the keys for sustainable development.

(4) They should work more intensively with the groups of predelinquents and disadvantaged people like street children, rag-pickers, scavengers, backward classes and lower castes. It will serve two purposes. These groups will learn more environmental friendly strategies and they will also get special attention which is required from social justice and human rights' angle.

(5) Social worker should start a crusade against religious and ritualistic practices which pollute water by putting flowers, candles and even dead bodies in to it. Polluting air in the name of religious rituals should also be minimized. Raising voice against religious activities is difficult, but social worker can use their 'warm and friendly professional relationship' in the community.

(6) Social workers and social activists should also pressurize the industries which are preparing dangerous items and releasing untreated waste in the water. There are countless examples of this type of production. To mention a few G.P. Ice factory run by Jyothindra Gandhi started producing ice of red and brown colour because of untreated garbage dumped in the backyard of the factory. Its liquid reached the ground water which got polluted. Due to that untreated waste of a neighbouring chemical factory chemical ice was produced. In the next case, tanneries of North Arcot district created havoc i.e. chrome is discharged by tanneries. Now chrome has infected even mothers' milk in that area. It means that a child gets chrome as the first diet. People have accepted skin eruption and boils as usual things. Third example is very alarming. Karjat Taluka in Maharashtra shows an incident of reducing average life span among tribals. In 1950, it was 55 years and now it has come to 35 years.[31] These are harmful impacts of the modern technology and social workers should develop pressure group among masses. Social worker should also raise voice against dangerous tribal practices like jhoom cultivation and burning cowdung as fuel.

(7) They should help people to come out of poverty and poverty culture. Redistribution of productive resources should be the first target of social workers and social activists. Poverty forces the masses to think of present meal or at

the most the next meal. Therefore future planning is not possible for poverty striken masses. Ultimately poverty psyche results in natural resource exploitation because the philosophy of investment for future appears somewhat utopian to a poor person.

(8) Social workers should work with the largest group of disadvantaged population i.e. the women, both as a deprived group and also as a potential provider of assistance and care to other deprived groups. In spite of so much illiteracy, lack of health care and nutrition, non-inheritance of property and lower status, women have fought as Chipko activists in the past. Not only this, they also got united to fight against alcoholism, in Saharanpur, Haryana and Chattisgarh.[32]

(9) Another possible role of social workers is acquainting people with the available facts and informations such as:

a) Greatest famine in China during 1959-60 spread due to dogmatic and inflexible plans. It ultimately led to the death of 20 million.[33]

b) During the last century sea level rose approximately 0.12–0.15 metres. It is going to be 0.6 high metres within another century. Perhaps the West Antarctic ice sheet will break up and will melt rapidly.[34]

c) In just one year of structural adjustment in 1990-91, 22 million people have been pushed into poverty.[35]

These and similar informations should be shared with the people so that they should take all precautions.

A professional social worker is not aiming towards a utopian world of 'no interference with the nature'. He appreciates 'minimum interference' with nature because 'no interference' is not possible. The moment treatment system of sick and ailing was evolved, interference was started. Treatment and cure multiplied the population and so many problems were started in a series. At present, social worker knows that large cities, industries and modern life style will continue. Electricity, irrigation and chemical products will exist in future also. But he also realises that the planet can be saved, only when every step is planned very carefully. In this process social worker can work as a link between government and public.

As a matter of fact, social worker/social activist would have a much more meaningful and vital role in managing sustainable development in future. The coming century will clear all our doubts and remove all our hesitations regarding controlled economic development which will emerge in place of ruthless economic development of today. Hopefully it will not be too late by then!

NOTES

1. Rusi Engineer, "Looking back on the 80s and Forward to the 90s" *Sanctuary,* Vol. X, No. 2, 1990, p. 34–35.
2. Kanta Prasad, "Social Development in Drought Prone Areas — Policy Issues and Options". *The Indian Journal of Public Administration*, (New Delhi: IIPA. Vol XXXIX, No. 3, July–September 1993), p. 457.
3. M.N. Buch, "Afforestation Utterances Deforestation Policies", *Sanctuary* Vol. IX, No. 3, 1989, p. 75.
4. B.B. Vohra, "Confusion on the Forestry Front", *Sanctuary,* Vol. VII, No. 3, 1988, p. 67.
5. *Ibid*. p. 64.
6. Walter A. Rosenbaum, *Environmental Politics and Policy*, II Edition (New Delhi: Affiliated East West Press Pvt. Ltd., 1991), p. 52.
7. *Ibid*. p. 39.
8. *Ibid*. p. 305.
9. Dogra, *Encyclopedia of Development, Environment and Welfare* (New Delhi: 1995), p. 115.
10. *Ibid*.
11. *Ibid*. p. 189–190.
12. World Rivers Review May 1995 quoted by Dogra *Encyclopedia of Development Environment & Welfare*, p. 196.
13. *Ibid*. 196–197.
14. Rusi Engineer, Looking Backward on the 80s and Forward to 90s, in *Sanctuary,* Vol. X, No. 21, 1990, p. 40.
15. Gadgil quoted by Rusi Engineer, in *Sanctuary* p. 36.
16. Editorial *Down to Earth* (New Delhi: Centre for Science and Environment, 41, Tughlakabad Institutional Area Vol. 4, No. 16, January 15, 1996), p. 4.
17. Rusi Engineer, Looking Back on the 80s and Forward to the 90s, *Sanctuary,* Vol. X, No. 2, p. 46.
18. *Ibid*. p. 37.
19. *The United Nations and Human Rights* (New York: U.N.

Dept. of Public Information, 1984), p. 234.
20. V.T. Thamilmaran, *Human Rights in Third World Perspective* (New Delhi: Har Anand Publication 1992), p. 167.
21. *Ibid.* p. 169.
22. Founex Report quoted by V.T. Thamilmaran, *Human Rights in Third World Perspective*, p. 169–170.
23. Ravi Sharma, "Role of the Problem", in *Down to Earth* p. 5
24. *Ibid.*
25. V.T. Thamilmaran, *Human Rights in Third World Perspective*, p. 128.
26. Karel Vasak, quoted by Thamilmaran in *Human Rights in Third World Perspective*, p. 129.
27. Rusi Engineer, Looking Backward in 80s Forward in 90s, *Sanctuary*, p. 36.
28. R.R. Singh, "World Summit on Social Development — The Indian Case" in *Whither Social Development,* Edited by R.R. Singh, (Delhi: ASSWI 1995), p. 43.
29. Joke Schrijvers, (Translated by Linpugh) *The Violence of Development* (New Delhi: International Book Utrecht the Netherland & Kali for Women, 1993), p. 26.
30. *Ibid.*
31. Claude Alvares, *Social Development and Violence* (New Delhi: Oxford University Press, 1992), p. 26–28.
32. Dogra, *Encyclopedia of Development Environment and Welfare* p. 58-59.
33. *Ibid.* p. 80.
34. *Ibid.* p. 190.
35. Times of India quoted by Dogra, in *Encyclopedia,* p. 145.

CHAPTER VI

SUSTAINABLE DEVELOPMENT: A DIFFERENT ORIENTATION

The last two decades of this century have witnessed some crucial events like the fall of Eastern Europe, unification of Germany, nuclear experiments and over all rise in political conflicts and terrorism. The fall of communist block has created power imbalance. As a matter of fact, Uncle Sam has become the head of the global family now. Today it is very difficult to ignore the opinion of USA on any international matter. As a result every developing country wants to make place in the good books of USA. Due to this situation economic growth is considered more important than social development. But all these efforts are futile, because poverty is growing. As N.D. Jayal points out "Poverty, the most important threat to human survival, due to scarcity of essential resources, has increased in every part of the world. This is particularly true for all these cultures which were not based on large scale trade and commerce."[1]

We see that GNP based development is soaked in blood. It is a systematic violence against trees, rivers, animals, humans, natural resources and social justice. This is taking us towards poverty and deprivation. There is a constant pressure on the developing countries to have more production and more national income. We see that countries producing more oil, gas or coal are occupying top positions in all the international forums. For example, Arabic is an accepted language in the conferences of UNO, whereas Hindi, Urdu, etc. are totally ignored by UN authorities though they are spoken in large areas. In this atmosphere developing countries cannot be blamed if they are trying to join the rat race. In fact many of them want to leave no stone unturned for making place in the list of developed countries. They try out all the possible welfare and developmental measures in their countries. They feel that these measures will improve their standard of living and reduce their poverty level. However at the conceptual level, efforts for sustaining development are also appreciated.

Bottlenecks in the Process of Sustainable Development

Irony is that, some welfare and development measures are supporting and enhancing the process of violence. GATT (General Agreement on Traffic and Trade), TNCs (Transnational Corporations), MTO (Multilateral Trade Organisation) are now active and they have elements of violence and exploitation inherent in them. Their latest sensation is IPR (Intellectual Property Rights). It appears as if it provides protection to all innocent rural and tribal people. Their folk art, culture and medicines may even be made patent in the name of tribal and rural folk. But in actual practice it may be harmful in some ways. There are certain limitations. It will commercialise old practices and create certain complication e.g. it will make traditional healers like *Neem* paste, *Tulsi* or Turmeric very expensive. Moreover, it will take knowledge to Transnational Corporations which means there will be shift from common to private rights. In that case 'priority' (what ever it might be) will be given to only those discoveries which are profitable for industrial application. Small scale, informal or domestic practices will receive no attention. As Vandana Shiva remarks, "Most innovations by women are for domestic, local and public use not for international trade, MNCs innovate for the sole purpose of increasing their share in global market and international trade; and TRIPs in GATT will only enforce MNCs' rights to monopolise all production, distribution and profits at the cost of all citizens and small producers worldwide."[2] Now due to some changes, farmers' right to save seeds of a new variety is curtailed. It is possible that seeds and knowledge may be obtained by paying royalty which means that ultimately rich countries will possess every knowledge and eventually produce only commercially profitable crops and destroy biodiversity. At this point it is very difficult to assess whether IPR is a favour to tribals, farmers and traditional people or it is a curse for them.

One important but less emphasised feature of sustainable development is women's contribution in development specially in sustainable development. Consistently women's role in preserving ecology and keeping the traditional practices alive, is ignored. It is noteworthy that women should not be taken as a deprived needy group (or handicappeds?), they should be taken as beneficiaries, participants, providers and planners of development; just like men. Women's issues are somewhat neglected in India but private groups and NGOs are projecting women as protectors of natural balance and environment. People like Vandana Shiva have discussed a lot about the role of women as parallel to mother nature. But Government is indifferent towards this. It is launching new schemes for the promotion and upliftment of women but their role as protectors of nature and environment is totally ignored by the planners. Therefore, their participation in sustainable development is also overlooked by the authorities. This means that at the academic level there is some awakening regarding eco-feminism but in actual practice right perspective has not been evolved so far. 'Mainstreaming' women in developmental process should be the present strategy. It means development of women's capacities and contribution and linking them to the macro developmental issues such as poverty, food scarcity, overcrowding and urbanization. It also means that gender dimension should be included in all development programmes, plans and models. Nevertheless, we find that mainstreaming the women has been ignored in India and precisely in all the third world countries. Here a table is given to show the gradual shift in the approach. However, still a lot more is required to be done (see table on p. 78).[3]

In this connection, environmentalists feel that woman was trying to maintain the ecological balance because she was working as food (fodder, fuel and water) gatherer and man was working as hunter in the stone age and today also as engineer and scientist he is 'hunting' the ecological balance and 'killing' the natural resources. It will not be irrelevant if we find the outcome of similar studies in the other depressed countries. We see that in simple and indigenous societies the role of women is that of a protector of nature, family and society.

How the work is divided.[4]
(Africa, percentage of total labour in hours)

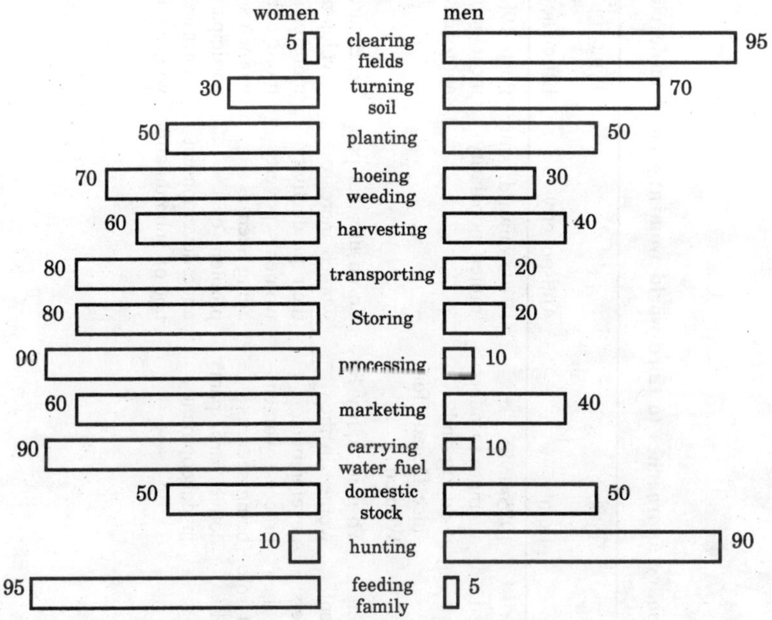

Source: FAO/FTPP publication; *Restoring the balance*, 1992.

This diagram clearly indicates that throughout the dark continent women have adopted a nurturing approach which has no place for any kind of violence; whereas it is contrary in the case of men. Back home, the situation is almost the same. Non-violent role of women, as special contribution to sustainable development, is now understood by environmentalist but ignored by many others. Here it is worth mentioning that Chipko in North, Apko in the South and anti-liquor

Different policy approaches to third-world women: women-in-development (WID)

		Type I		Type II	Type III
Issuess	Welfare	Equity	Anti-poverty	Efficiency	Empowerment
Period most popular	1950–1970: but still widely used	1975–1985: attempts to adopt it during and since Decade for Women	1970s onward: still limited popularity	Post- 1980s: now most popular approach	1975 onward: accelerated during 1980s, still limited popularity
Purpose	To bring women into development as better mothers: this is seen as their most important role in development	To gain equity for women in the development process: women being seen as active participants in devepment	To ensure that poor women increase their productivity: women's poverty being seen as problem of underdevelopment not of subordination	To ensure that development is more efficient and more effective, women's economic participation being seen as associated with equity	To empower women through greater self-reliance: women's subordination being seen not only as problem of men but also of colonial and neo-colonial oppression

Needs of women met and roles recognized	To meet PGN in reproductive role, relating particularly to food aid, malnutrition and family planning	To meet SGN in terms of triple role—directly through state top-down intervention giving political and economic autonomy by reducing inequality with men	To meet PGN in productive role, to earn an income, particularly in small-scale income generating projects	To meet PGN in context of declining social services by relying on all three roles of women and elasticity of women's time	To reach SGN in terms of triple role—indirectly through bottom-up mobilization around PGN—as means of confronting oppression

Source: Caroline O.N. Moser, "Gender planning in the third world: meeting practical and strategic gender needs," World Development, vol. 17, No. 11 (1989).

Notes: PGN: Practical gender needs (those needs formulated from the concrete conditions women experience, in their engendered position within the sexual division of labour, and deriving out of this practical gender interests for human survival).

SGN: Strategic gender needs (those needs formulated from the analysis of women's subordination to men, and deriving out of this the strategic gender interest identified for an alternative, more equal and satisfactory organization of society).

campaign of women in Uttara Khand, Chattisgarh and Nellore (in A.P.) are the examples of their nurturing role for trees rivers, animals and humans. These movements also show the care and concern among women's voluntary groups for sustainable development. At the same time these struggles indicate a new sense of awakening, strength, unity and self worth among them. But in the government sector, their participation in environment preservation is by and large ignored. The document released by the Department of Women & Child Development, Ministry of Human Resource Development, Govt. of India, New Delhi in 1995 does not include any thing to promote the special role of the women in the movement of environment preservation and sustainable development. Though it includes almost all other areas. This negligence is harmful as well as dangerous. Hence, it is not only important for the planners, but also for all the concerned people, to realise the importance of women's contributions. Vandana Shiva has written in her famous book "Sustenance.... is built on the continued capacity of nature to renew its forests fields and rivers. These resource systems are intrinsically linked in life producing and life conserving cultures and it is in managing the integrity of ecological cycles in forestry and agriculture that women's productivity has been most developed and evolved. Women transfer fertility from the forests to the field and to animals. They transfer animal waste as fertilisers for crops and crops' byproducts to animals as fodder. This partnership between women's and nature's work ensures the sustainability of sustenance and it is this critical partnership that is torn as under when the project of development becomes patriarchal project, threatening both nature and women."[5]

This tender and artistic role of the women in sustainable development has been recognised by some international organizations e.g. in 1987 Right Livelihood Foundation Stockholm award was given to the women involved in Chipko movement. But in India this recognition is conspicuously absent atleast in the government plans and policies. It creates a serious drawback and sometimes it appears that all concerned people and NGOs are fighting against the government and government is having an alliance with the greedy industrialists and contractors who are out to destroy environment and eventually sustainable development too.

Another comparatively neglected feature of sustainable development is global economic justice. It has been felt that all the benefits of development are basically going to the developed and industrial countries. There is injustice everywhere, whether it is between rich and poor countries or between rich and poor sections of the same country. During the past five decades world income increased sevenfold (in reality GDP and income per person more than tripled in per capita GDP). But this growth has been highly unequal. Between 1960 and 1991 the share of the world income for the richest 20% of the global population rose from 70% to 85% while the share of the poorest 20% declined from 2.3% to 1.4%. The poorest 20% people of the world had a 0.9% share in world trade, 1.1% share in world investment, 0.9% in world saving and 0.2% share in commercial credit.[6] (See chapter I also).

This description is self-explanatory. But it is quite clear that injustice prevails every where. Dogra has written "The belief that in general, various development efforts or activities create opportunities in which all can share, is not rooted in reality. In an unequal society, only those members who have already reached a certain level can claim a share in new opportunities. On the other hand, the possibility always exists that the adverse effects have to be borne by precisely those members who are unable to have the new opportunities."[7] At this point we feel that the former colonies of Africa and Asia are still facing slavery and serfdom. Not only that, poor countries sometimes get waste of harmful products or hazardous goods. As Dogra has said, "A society may be clever enough to avoid endangering its own resource base but it may export its environmental cost to some helpless poor societies by exploiting its strong position in the international policies and trade."[8] Examples are Bhopal gas tragedy, dumping nuclear waste in Australian sea-shores and heaping the chemical drum in some remote villages of Nigeria.[9] Another horrifying example comes into limelight after the enquiry of Green peace and Indian government organization *Srishti*. They found that ".... each Indian port is an open door to the worst waste on the planet, in particular from United States, Australia and Canada .... *Srishti*, in the port of Bombay, Calcutta and Madras, found that 151 importers have brought in over the last two years more than 66,000 cubic tons of zinc and lead in the form of ash, residue, and toxic slag from 49 countries."[10] This is an irony that those who are so much concerned about environment in their own countries are shamelessly depositing their garbage around our ports. Inspite of a lot of verbocily about human rights and social justice, in reality, they are practicing colonialism and spreading serfdom in the Third World.

Here mentioning WHO's report will be relevant which says "In the poor countries life expectancy is little above 40 while in richest countries it approaches 80. Life expectancy is actually decreasing in some of the poorest countries and vaccination rates are falling."[11] This situation looks like a conspiracy of the developed nations.

The WHO says that inequality in health situation is growing between countries, between well off and disadvantaged groups within countries and between sexes. The whole description makes us think that sustainable development is not possible without eradicating or atleast minimizing global injustice.

After the global injustice and inequality the issue of population explosion must be taken as another central issue for sustainable development. R.E. Mum describes population growth as an on-going phenomenon. At the same time there is an inverse relationship between economic development and environmental quality. These three factors may be represented as shown in the figure.[12]

The graph is quite clear in itself. Population keeps growing, proving Malthusian theory. On the other hand, economic development also takes place gradually but ultimately uncontrolled economic growth causes deterioration in the quality of environment. It means, economic growth (if not planned) may lead to environmental bankruptcy. It is evident that this bankruptcy will take the whole society towards 'sustainable deprivation and poverty' (see figure on p. 83).

Population Development and Environment

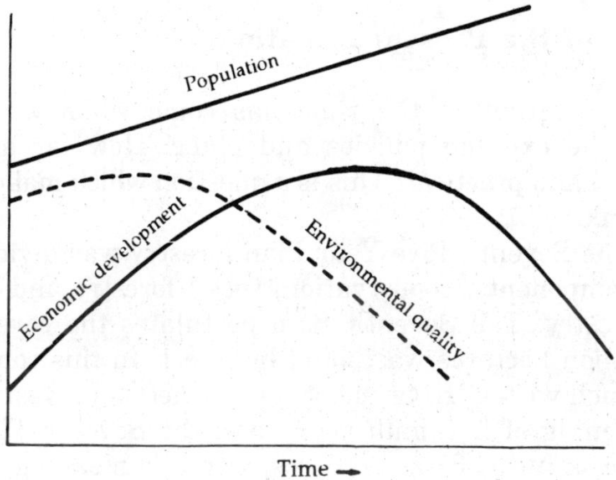

Schematic representation of the predicament of developing countries.
Development 1989:2/3 — Journal of SID

There is no doubt that there is some awareness over this issue. Not only this, a commission headed by Harlan Brundtland (Prime Minister of Norway and Chairperson of the World Commission on Environment and Development) was appointed. Moreover World Industry Conference on Environmental Management and many other similar bodies have been doing some work but the net result is somewhat disappointing. Common man in developing countries, has been generally unconcerned regarding environmental issues. Nobody has given up chemical fertilizers, plastic bags and fridges (which produce CFCs) inspite of the knowledge of their harmful effects. Green revolution, white revolution, development of monoculture (loss of biodiversity) and establishment of pharmaceutical industries are also going ahead in full swing and in most of the cases without taking necessary precautions. It is quite possible that due to population explosion situation will worsen in future. GATT, IPR, MNCs, gender bias, global injustice and population problems are some of less considered issues so far in the scenario of sustainable development. But they are central and important issues particularly in the third world context. In India more attention should be paid on them. Inspite of that future appears to be quite bleak if steps are not taken immediately.

Review of the Present Situation

In Indian situation the time has come when we should review the existing policies and plans. How far are they beneficial and practical? This is a question which makes every one think.

In the Seventh Five Year Plan forestry was divided into three components, conservation, social forestry and production forestry. The Seventh Plan postulates the coverage of five million hectares wasteland by forest. In this connection M.N. Buch writes "In terms of the per hectare investment in the greening of five million hectare, the Seventh Plan provides for only Rs. 37.20. The cost of really meaningful plantation is about Rs. 10,000 per hectare which means that the plan outlay is about 270 times less than required."[13] Alongwith this fault, some other points are also there e.g. the claim of 50 million hectare wasteland identified by Wasteland Development Board is also nothing but degraded forests. Otherwise all cultivable land has been given on *patta* to landless people under 20 point programme. At some places social forestry is at the cost of reserved forests. Moreover, target oriented plantation is attempted in xerophylic conditions and there is no aftercare also. Buch feels, "Conservation rather than plantation, adequate funding of programme for preservation and enhancement of designated forests, participative forestry to meet village *nistar* requirement, regulated grazing, pasture development...must form the planks of our afforestation policy."[14]

It is not only forest policies but also dam construction policies which create serious hurdles. Gold Smith has been out spoken. He remarks "... dam in USA were being built largely because the State paid for them. Now the law has changed and requires the local communities to contribute. So dam building too has come to an end in USA and the industry keeps going largely by persuading Third World countries to buy these highly destructive and totally uneconomic devices."[15] This is not the only example. In Egypt Aswan dam created many ecological problems. There were so many diseases because germs found shelter in the stored water. Floods were stopped which used to bring fertile soil. Why all these consequences were there? Only in the name of progress. But what is this progress? The close associate of 'development' are destruction of social and ecological system, increase in accidents, mental diseases, suicides, crime, drug abuse and child prostitution etc. Are these the salient features of progress and development? Obviously environment destruction is not the only outcome of development. There are many other serious side effects too.

One should remember that sustainable development does not depend on forests only. There are many more factors which contribute to development, Misra wrote at one place, "It involves far more than environment-friendly technology. It involves paradigm change, it involves change in style of development, it involves change in our attitude, and it involves political, social and ethical changes."[16] Much of the unplanned and ruthless development has taken place due to lack of knowledge and human greed. Forests were destroyed for crop growing. Ozone layer was depleted because fertilizers and fridges were needed and underground water was misused because irrigation was required. In other words, faulty development was planned to help the poor but on the contrary, "Poverty, environment and development are interrelated .... Poverty is a major cause as well as effect of global environment problem."[17] Efforts to remove or reduce poverty should not bring more poverty in the long run. But unfortunately this has happened in many cases in the past.

Conclusion

It is important to note that nature and the earth are not commodities to be used for personal greed. Authorities should always remember that the first right of the products and natural resources should be given to the sons of the soil and ethnic groups. Migration of refugees or displacement of indigenous people is against the spirit of sustainable development. Here, this can also be added that totally foreign technologies which are not in harmony with the existing systems are not only costly but harmful too. In this context one must remember once again that there is a relationship among various activities, programmes and schemes. Local activities have far reaching effects. As Elvis Thomas says that the idea of development "encompasses every aspect not only of human life but also of surrounding elements as well."[18]

One has to take environmental issues as critical issues which are going to decide the future and fate of the planet. This crisis has immediate, as well as, far reaching effects. Most important point of consideration is preparation of properly defined and practice oriented plans. Implementation of such plans must involve those who are going to suffer directly due to environment exploitation. These suffers may include housewives, tribals, farmers, slum dwellers, snake charmers, fisher men and sailors etc. Without their active involvement and participation ecological movement which is the backbone of sustainable development, can not become meaningful and result oriented.

Here, one should not forget the element of gross injustice inherent in the present programmes of commercialized development. We borrow the resources of future though we neither have inclination nor possibility of returning them to the future generations. Today they have no capacity to stop us because they are either small or non existent. They have no power to impress upon as vote banks. Decision makers of today will not be there to face acid rains, global warming, ozone layer depletion, growing deserts, extinction of species and total socio economic disorganization. Brundtland Commission gave the message that the problem of environment is linked to the problem of poverty, underdevelopment and over population. This, has been a century of scientific and technological growth even then there have never been so many poor, homeless, illiterate and unemployed people in the past.

Internationalism and multilateralism should be the approach of ecological movement. The whole planet has a common future and fate. Global interdependence should be managed collectively.

The most important change is required in the accounting system. The environmental damage, which is created for achieving higher GNP should be deducted from GNP

Valuewise, national resources also have a price. Development should also include the price of resources harvesting and extraction. If the resources are exploited due to unsustainable management then it will lose future benefits. In that case the said resources will have a different way of measuring their costs which is called users cost. Therefore all the natural resources have extraction costs, environmental costs and users cost at the same time. This is why they are much more valuable then their market price. The finished products of any industry should pay for environment cleaning according to its polluting tendency.

In fact all the developmental projects must have environment budget. They should invest some thing in the environment. This pricing measurement should help us change our project formulation and resource allocation system. This should also change our definition of economic development. Diminishing social return of growth-and gross inequality will also be reduced with this technique.

No doubt it is a massive task and precious time has been wasted so far but now we should start programme of sustainable development with full force. Presumably social workers will have a significant role in this movement.

NOTES

1. N.D. Jayal, *Alternative Strategies for Development* (New Delhi: Intach, National Trust for Art & Culture Heritage, Lodhi Estate 1992), p. 1.
2. Mara Mies and Vandana Shiva, *Ecofeminism* (New Delhi: Kali for Women, 1993), p. 239.
3. *Women 2000* UN Publications, Austria, Vienna International Centre, p. 6.
4. Bruce Cabarle and Aaron Zaneta Gainuig Grond, "People's Participation in Tropical Action Plan for Equador in Forest Trees and People", *News Letter* No. 15/16, February 1992 Sweden Swedish University of Agricultural Science (SUAS), p. 37.
5. Vandana Shiva, *Staying Alive* (New Delhi: Kali for Women 1992), p. 45.
6. HDR 1993 quoted by Bharat Dogra, *Encyclopaedia of Devel-*

opment, Environment and Welfare (New Delhi: 1995), p. 31.

7. Dogra, *Encyclopaedia of Development, Environment and Welfare* (New Delhi: 1995), p. 25.
8. Dogra, p. 28.
9. C.B.S.C., Interact in English Class X (New Delhi: CBSC, 1994), p. 71.
10. AFP, *The Hindustan Times,* New Delhi: Wednesday, July 17, 1996, p. 14.
11. WHOs report quoted by Dogra, in *Encyclopaedia of Development, Environment and Welfare*, p. 25.
12. R.E. Munn, "Towards Sustainable Development an Environmental Perspective", in *Development,* SID 1989, p. 70.
13. M.N. Buch, "Afforestation Utterances Deforestation Policies", *The Sanctuary*, Vol. IX, No. 3, 1989, p. 71.
14. *Ibid*. p. 77.
15. Gold Smith quoted by Kamala Chowdhry, "Poverty Environment and Development", *Sanctuary* Vol. X, No. 1, 1989, p. 77.
16. R.P. Mishra, "Sustainable Development: Ecological Perspective", in *Indian Journal of Public Administration* (New Delhi: Vol. XXXIX No. 3, July–September 1993), p. 257.
17. Kamla Chowdhry, "Poverty Environment and Development" in *Indian Journal of Public Administration*, p. 79.
18. Elvis Thomas, Sustainable Development, *Perspectives in Social Work*, Nirmala Vikas Journal. (Bombay: No. 3, Vol. X, 1996), p. 4.